Acknowledgements

MW00903017

If not for the following people and resources my book would have remained a memory.

I am deeply indebted to my cousin Sue Miller, who has been like a sister to me. She was one of the most beautiful women I've ever had the pleasure of knowing, both inside and out. Sue was an inspiration to me personally and professionally.

I'd like to thank my editor, Vicki Tosher from ONE LAST LOOK. I appreciate her kindness, patience, and guidance.

I am grateful to my daughter Diane, who not only has worked with me from the beginning and was a tremendous help of inspiration and encouragement. She even shared some of her memories of escapades from earlier years that I had forgotten. I'm thankful to Gail for her by-the-book coaching whose thoughtful input was invaluable, and level-headed Mark who keeps my feet planted and for just being here.

Thank you to my step daughter, Felicia Baumel and her two daughters, Shera and Izzie. Thanks to my sister, Joan Micklin Silver.

Special thanks to my lawyer and friend Larry Morten, and his wife Karen for putting up with all the phone calls. and the late Warren Zweiback who kept me out of the poor house.

I will always appreciate Ozzie Nogg, for pointing me in the right direction. My cousin Larry Koom, and his father, Morrie; they just don't get much finer.

My gratitude to Eunie Denenberg: when I came home from my marriage to a con artist, she helped me reinvent myself and find my way. Thank you to Rosemary Teckmeyer who has been a true-blue friend with a great sense of humor. I will always be indebted to Opal Adams for her tireless and unselfish guidance, Lou for his wise words, and Carolyn Gilreath, who never did keep her distance. Thanks to the YWCA who helped me survive scary nights and lonely days.

Many thanks to my assistants: Danna who read and re-read my early drafts, and made valuable recommendations.

Love and thanks to Carl Watson for his kindness, patience, wisdom and most of all his friendship. I wish it had been more years, my friend. Marlene Rollins, thank you for letting me be one of your friends. And last but not least thank you James McKay for the many talks, letters and years with you as my adviser. You can take any topic and turn it into a well-written story.

Introduction

Those of us with a handicap are more vulnerable to exploitation than those who are not. I suffer from Retinitis Pigmentosa; a degenerative eye disease that causes severe vision impairment and often blindness. Science and medical technology trumpet breakthroughs in treatment regularly, but nothing ever seems to pan out. At least for me.

In my early fifties, I met and married my third husband, a virile, charismatic sheriff. Life with Cooper could be idyllic. He lavished me with verbal roses: "You have a brilliant mind." "You're my woman, the only one I've ever loved." "I can't live without you." He made little things romantic. He'd hold my hand as we sat on the screened-in porch listening to a gentle summer rain, and make me feel safe from harm as we rode his horse double in the moonlight. Taking my hand, he'd lead me down the steps to point out the first purple crocus that peeked through the snow or make a spur-of-the-moment decision to drive hundreds of miles out of the way so I could see Mt. Rushmore – one of my favorite landmarks – before my vision diminished further.

Any glimmer of hope for a loving relationship was short-lived. There was a callousness to Cooper that erupted on increasingly frequent occasions. As the bonds of our marriage weakened, I saw more and more of his other face, the one he concealed until he could get away with showing it.

Love and hate can be equally disastrous. I had to revisit my past before I could comprehend why I was reliving it. Only then would I begin to heal.

Prologue

After driving several hours across the hot plains, cradled in the crook of my new husband's arm, Cooper pulled into a rest stop near the foothills hemming Yellowstone National Park.

We strolled and stretched before getting back on the road. Cooper took a pleasure detour to enjoy the scenic drive along a river shown on a map. As the back road began to twist and turn, the blue sky took on strings of white zigzagging jet trails and high-altitude cirrus clouds. The afternoon acquired a subtle evening hue, and we rolled down the windows to enjoy the cool mountain air, rife with the smells of pine and sage from the river valley below.

The last bars of sunlight were disappearing into twilight, the time of day my vision is worst. The world seemed dark green to me, like moss covering a river bank.

I heard whitewater rapids echoing from steep cliffs where the canyon narrows. Cooper pointed out deer standing in deep shadows, saying he wished I could see the panorama of natural beauty. As for me, I commented on the grace of the whitetail. The truth is because it was dusk, and with the gradual loss of my vision, I couldn't see it if it was a grizzly bear standing on our bumper. Sometimes I fibbed; Cooper had reached the point where he occasionally lost patience with my failing vision.

He lifted his arm and stretched to relieve the stiffness in his back. He had had surgery at the Mayo Clinic after he rolled his cruiser during a high-speed chase. That was before our marriage. After a year in traction, he resumed his duties as the elected sheriff. In addition to being a large man whose nickname was "Bear," he had a lot of political pull in his county.

Cooper said, "Jake called while you were packing. We're invited to a barbecue of T-bones and baked potatoes."

"I heard that Jake beats Ann. Count me out."

Cooper paused in mid-country music channel surf: static, news and commercials, and yelled, "Don't you dare make a derogatory remark about my friend!" He whipped the car onto a gravel turnout, rocks pinging against the undercarriage.

Now, I'd done it. In the fury-charged silence, the wild waters crashed against rocks in the gorge below. We had stopped at the edge of a precipice.

"I'm sorry," I cringed. "Please don't be angry."

Cooper had a pearl-handled Derringer concealed in his boot and a .45 caliber automatic handgun under the seat. He wouldn't use them against me, would he? The proximity of firearms, his rage, and the isolation of the wilderness raised my heart rate. I sweated profusely. I feared that his increasingly violent outbursts over the past eighteen months would cross the line to physical violence.

He pinned me against the seat and forced open my door. At 6'4" and pushing 240 pounds, his bulk crushed my chest. "Get out!"

Panic twisted my insides. What were my odds of survival? I was terrified of the rugged, unforgiving canyon just beyond the guardrail. Knowing I would never survive, I became hysterical. I clutched the seat.

"Cooper, please don't leave me here. It's almost dark. You know I can't see."

"You should have thought about that before you opened your big mouth."

The snarling sound of wild waters echoed up the ravine.

"OUT!"

PART ONE

One

My friend Margo and I, both recently divorced – she from her third husband, and I from my second (Donald the skirt-chaser) – had been discussing ways to re-enter the singles scene. Margo, feeling more adventurous than I, called one afternoon, exuberant. "I've discovered a man mine of unlimited potential! *The Hookup* is filled with ads of available men. We can each create our profiles. Best part – it's anonymous."

"Do you mean the personals?" I asked nervously.

"Yes. We'll be reading résumés to find a good man."

"But the personals can be phony – full of lies," I objected.

"This is just a way to meet men. We don't have to marry them."

My stomach churned as my insecurities surfaced. What if no one likes me? "I don't think I'm ready."

"Of course, you are," Margo insisted. "You didn't want to take ballroom dance lessons. Look how much fun we had. Now we're ready for dance partners."

"You had fun," I thought. The instructor favored you because of your sassy cha-cha.

Margo continued to pressure, "This is the perfect solution for both of us. I'm so busy working on my degree. And let me tell you, school is no place to meet men. They're all too busy with their lives. And I don't have time for singles functions. The classifieds will be an easier way to work around your visual difficulties."

"So, what you're saying, is, they'll fall for me before I literally fall over them."

We laughed.

Coping with my eyesight has been a struggle since childhood. My first symptom was night blindness. Because I played kickball and tag at sundown, I was always covered with bruises. My parents attributed these scrapes to clumsiness. Halloween was especially scary – not because of ghosts and goblins. My younger sisters, Joany and Carol, ran ahead, anxious to fill their sacks with candy before curfew. I was left behind trampling flower beds and running into fences and other trick-or-treaters. When I was eight, Mom and Dad took me to a series of physicians seeking an explanation for my awkwardness. Our last appointment was with Dr. August, an ophthalmologist who wore a white lab coat, reminding me not to blink as he shined a bright penlight directly into my pupils. After several tests, he diagnosed Retinitis Pigmentosa, a degenerative eye disease and informed my parents, "Your daughter's eyesight will deteriorate at an indeterminate rate. She may eventually go blind." Mom and Dad were devastated, perhaps envisioning raising Helen Keller for the rest of their lives. Although my parents exhausted every available measure to slow the progression, they never discussed my eye disease with me, as if not talking about it would make it go away. Thus, they minimized the family's concern about the seriousness of the condition.

I started wearing glasses and was taken for annual field tests to check my peripheral vision, which decreased over the years. My only restriction was playing outside at night; I had to watch from the sidelines. I didn't like being left out of the neighborhood games, but since I was able to read my favorite books, ride my bike and attend school with my friends, I wasn't concerned.

I was growing tired of Margo micromanaging my life, but perhaps she was right. The personals might work to my advantage. Not having to navigate dark, smoky bars with loud, pulsating music and faceless weirdoes reeking of booze would give me an edge. The phone could weed out losers. I wasn't going to find a date sitting in my living room, so I decided to go for it. I looked forward to starting anew and fantasized about my true love, who would be attentive and spontaneous in the bedroom. My virile Harlequin man had no specific features. Nightly ravishment was a given. We would enjoy hours of scintillating conversation, sharing our innermost thoughts and feelings.

I sat at my kitchen table, writing and rewriting sparkling self-descriptions, fudging my age and embellishing my attributes.

Classy, WF, fortyish, loves books, long walks, and laughter, looking for WM to spice up my life. If you are trustworthy and adventurous, I'm waiting to hear from you.

With the help of a magnifier, which I now required for reading, I scanned the profiles in *The Hookup* – a romantic shopping bazaar. As time passed, Margo and I traded dates like children trade baseball cards. It was safe, and we had a lot of fun and laughs. Soon I was dating two nice men. Neither gave me butterflies, but as Mother used to say, "Go out, you never know who you will meet." Within a few short months, both Hal and John mentioned marriage, but in my experience, nice men translated to boring.

I was hunting for a bad boy. He appeared eight months later.

Swirling snow painted the yard and trees as I stepped outside to get the mail. I sat down in the breakfast nook to sort through it, sipping a fresh cup of coffee. I was excited when I recognized an envelope with *The Hookup* logo. Hoping that this man would be "the one," I hurriedly ripped it open. His letter read:

> My name is Cooper. I am the sheriff of Marshall County and live on a farm, five miles from Woodland, Nebraska. My favorite pastimes are gardening and hunting. I want to get to know you. Call me.

> Enclosed was a copy of his ad and phone number.

> ***WM, 44, rugged outdoorsman, financially secure, honest, dependable, loves adventure and travel. Wants to send flowers and romance the right lady. If you like candlelight dinners and horseback rides in the moonlight, I'm all yours.***

My pulse quickened. The possibility of romance and adventure was intoxicating. I'd never dated anyone in law enforcement. How exciting could that be? I had grown up within the confines of my neighborhood, exposed only to men in starched shirts and some with personalities as stiff as their collars.

I could hardly contain my excitement as I dialed the sheriff. Days dragged by without an answer. I didn't give up. I grumbled to Margo, "If I can't reach him tomorrow, I'll go back to the personals." I tried one last time. Cooper answered.

"I'm glad you kept trying. I've been working rotating shifts."

"Tell me about yourself," I said, anxious to find out everything about him.

He laughed. "That might take a while. How about getting together?"

We made plans to meet at my house, in two weeks. Meeting a man on my turf would make it easier to hide my visual impairment – at least until after the first kiss. And it would be more convenient than arranging a ride to and from the neighborhood coffee shop. I had relinquished my driver's license during my second marriage when pedestrians, street lights, and stop signs were no longer in my line of vision, and I became a motorized deathtrap.

Cooper called at least twice a day prior to our date. He was witty and articulate, with a smooth, seductive voice. Why isn't this guy attached, I wondered? We never ran out of conversation. I couldn't wait to hear from him. Instead of talking about himself non-stop, like some men, he asked about me, making me feel like I mattered. I learned he was divorced with two sons and a daughter – all grown. I told him about my son Mark, my daughters Gail and Diane, and Abby, my stepdaughter to whom I had remained close after my divorce from her father. As the days wore on our conversations grew more personal, intimate, and affectionate.

Cooper had unpredictable boundaries; a man who walked on the wild side. He portrayed himself as "a hard-nosed lawman." I was ready for a taste of the wild myself. Having been a fan of fairy tales in childhood, it appeared that a bit of *Beauty and the Beast* was at work here. In between phone calls, I daydreamed about him. I slid in my Dolly Parton CD, *Save the Last Dance for Me,* which I had purchased because of his love of country music, and whirled around the house like a giddy teenager, fantasizing about our moonlight horseback rides and romantic candlelight dinners. I was falling in love.

As the evening of our first date approached, I was excited and nervous. Would our attraction continue once we met? I arranged a ride to the Rumor Mill to get my hair back to fabulous, then hurried home and carefully applied makeup. I dressed casually in a new pair of jeans and my favorite pink blouse. The doorbell rang. With much anticipation, I opened the front door. My heart sank. Standing before me was a dime store cowboy in a tan ten-gallon hat, ostrich skin boots, pointed at the toes, and a belt buckle the size of my mother's silver platter. I thought of Hoss Cartwright on the television series *Bonanza.* Cooper bore no resemblance to the rugged Marlboro Man I had envisioned. At 6'4" and weighing over 200 pounds, he was a giant. Square-jawed, with a high forehead. I noticed a prominent scar running from the center of his forehead to the corner of his left eyebrow. He had short red hair and penetrating clear blue eyes, the kind you wouldn't want to meet across an interrogation table. Trying to conceal my disappointment, I invited him in.

After sizing up the living room; leather sectional, marble coffee table, silk-shaded lamps, and large gold-framed paintings, his police-trained eyes focused on the grand piano. "This neighborhood is too rich for my blood. It reminds me of Beverly Hills. I almost kept driving."

Without missing a beat, I said. "It's character that counts, not trappings."

He smiled, "You'll be a challenge. Pretty and smart."

After pouring coffee I led Cooper to the family room, thinking he might feel more comfortable in an informal setting. I heard his boot drag on the tile. Sitting on the couch, he explained, "I have a slight limp because I was nearly killed in a high-speed chase. My cruiser flipped twice end-over-end. I broke my back."

I pictured the flashing red and blue lights, the siren blaring, and a cloud of dust trailing from his speeding patrol car. Just like in an action film on TV. "You could have been killed."

"I was in and out of hospitals for a year. I had surgery at Mayo Clinic. After my release, I caught up with the bastard."

Wow! This guy isn't afraid of anything. He didn't say what happened to the miscreant who put him in traction.

Cooper's direct way of talking had captivated me, and we had so much fun getting acquainted over the phone the past two weeks, but his appearance was a huge let-down compared to what I'd hoped for or expected. He was drawn to my 'bright mind' and ability to 'cut to the chase.' I was putty to his compliments.

He left at 11:00 p.m. No chemistry, but I hoped he'd call. My deep-rooted insecurity required that all potential boyfriends become smitten.

The phone rang at midnight. I was certain it was Hal, drunk again, calling from a bar to profess his undying love. I was surprised to hear Cooper's captivating voice. He had just arrived at his farm.

"I want to chase you," a pause on the line. "Do you want to be chased?"

Megavolts of electricity flowed through me. His confidence struck a chord with me, and I tried to keep my breathing steady. "By you, yes!" His words were so enticing and provocative that my first impression was forgotten. His come-at-you personality coupled with a straightforward chase-and-let-yourself-be-caught challenge was irresistible. I was ecstatic as I closed my eyes.

Two

On our second date, Cooper came to my 'Beverly Hills' mansion straight from shift. His eyes lit up when he saw me. I was delighted at how handsome and clean-cut he looked. There's something about a man in uniform. This attire was much more flattering than on the first date's. He walked tall and erect, proud of his profession. My physical attraction kicked in. He kissed me passionately, "You look nice and smell so good." I blushed, "You look pretty good yourself." He strode confidently into the house, his muscular arms full of firewood and two thick butcher's choice New York strips. I took the steaks to the kitchen, and he carried the logs into the family room. Too cold to grill outside, I broiled the meat in the oven. Anxious to make a good impression, I tried hard to conceal my discomfort. I could cook a decent meal; I just preferred not to spend a lot of time in the kitchen. His watchful eyes intensified my self-consciousness, but baked potatoes, garlic toast, and salad were effortless side dishes to prepare. Somehow, I avoided burning the steaks and singing my hair as I removed the meat from the oven. After dinner, Cooper complimented, "Those steaks were delicious."

Later, we sat in the family room with the lights dim. His hand found mine. He built a fire, and each time it started to die down, he stirred the embers and threw on another log. I watched his hands – strong and capable. I found him as easy to talk to as any man I had ever met. He was passionate about his farm. "You'd love country life. It's peaceful. The air is clean. There's nothing more thrilling than watching a field of corn grow from seed. When it rains, it means life. Wait till you see my vegetable garden this summer."

My stomach fluttered at the thought that he saw a future for us.

I shared my passion for reading. Not being a book lover, he only nodded. The romance was moving in the right direction. No sexual pass, no hurry, no mistakes needing correction. I was falling for a uniform with only a glimpse of the man.

Suddenly Cooper's mood turned dark, spoiling the romance. "I had a rotten childhood."

"What happened?" I asked, confused by the negative change in his demeanor. Until now we had been sharing compliments and good times: hayrack rides in the country and his favorite breakfast hangouts – Granny's and Jenny's.

He bit his lip. "My dad used to talk with his fists. When I was sixteen, he pushed me over the porch railing. It was December 24. I'd just gotten home from my job delivering flowers."

"That's terrible," I gasped. "Why would your father hurt you?"

Cooper gritted his teeth. "He was a mean drunk."

"What did your mother do?"

"Nothing. My parents divorced when I was fifteen. I lived with Dad; my younger brother, Grant, lived with Mom. I never got along with her either. She's a busybody, always snooping in my business."

My heart ached for Cooper. He had grown up in such a bitter household.

When I was sixteen, I was working at a women's clothing store, and spending my paychecks on clothes and movies at the Paramount Theater. Cooper appealed to my maternal instinct. On went my caretaker's hat. "You've been through so much," I said, picturing him as a frightened teenager. Little did I know that, through the years, his anger had turned to rage. "I wish there was something I could do."

"Erase my shitty childhood."

"I'll try." I would do anything to help Cooper overcome his violent past.

"Until I met you," he said squeezing my hand, "I didn't think the personals would work for me. I'm a lucky guy."

I thought of my parents.

My dad idolized my mother. As far as he was concerned, Mom could do no wrong. She oversaw the house and the endless demands of raising three daughters. Mom was proud of Dad's brilliant mind and admired his work ethic. He had built a successful lumber business. To see anything through his eyes was to watch it turn out profitably. Mom loved Dad, but I don't think she had the capacity to love him as deeply as he loved her. Possibly it was the way she and her siblings were raised. All three sisters were controlling and judgmental with unrealistic expectations of others.

Disagreements between my parents must have been hashed out behind closed doors. The few arguments I heard were low-volume sparrings at the dinner table. The conversation was ordinarily in English, but when the voices rose, or the subject grew unsuitable for young ears, my parents spoke in Yiddish, the language they learned as children in Bryansk and Gomel, Russia where they were born. Assuming that the topic must be interesting, I was a frustrated eavesdropper begging for translation. Although their discussions could be intense, there was no mention of divorce, no broken glass or black eye the next morning.

Cooper and I talked into the night in front of dancing flames. He didn't go home until 6:00 a.m. before the sun peaked over the horizon. He kissed me gently. His mouth was soft and warm. My whole body responded. That perfect evening is stamped in my memory forever.

On his next day off, the following week, Cooper invited me to see his farm. He wanted me to fall in love with it and cherish it as he did. It was time to come clean about my vision. I was afraid that my affliction might turn him off.

He was unperturbed by my revelation. "You have nothing to worry about," he said. "I'll take care of you."

"Good," I thought. "I trust this man. He cares." I felt safe.

It was a bright, sunny day in January and mild for Nebraska, when Cooper picked me up. En route he revealed, "The last gal I dated inherited a large sum of money and wanted to share by paying off the mortgage on my farm."

I was shocked. Speechless.

"Owen Tapp, the bank president, called and said that she'd sent a cashier's check."

"That is so generous."

"I wouldn't allow any woman to pay my way," Cooper scoffed. "I've worked my ass off for everything I own. I picked up the check and returned it, telling her the money would help put her seven-year-old daughter through college."

I was impressed with Cooper's unwillingness to accept money from a woman.

When we arrived at his farm, the snow kept us from exploring the grounds. We climbed the lopsided back steps and went directly inside. Taking my hand, he gave me a quick tour, which, because of its small scale, and meager furnishings, lasted about ten minutes. No need to linger in any of the rooms. The house was modest, dark, except the kitchen, which was bright. It smelled old; like a smokers' house. Our last stop was his bedroom. California King, better suited for his size, no headboard. An old beat up dresser with attached mirror that looked like it came from his youth. Dusty window air conditioner. I looked out the window, the view of the snow-covered fields; cattle grazing beyond the fence, a few of their white faces turned to stare at me. When I turned around, he was leaning against the door frame, arms crossed, head tilted to the right, His gaze was clear and blue. I couldn't take my eyes off him. Moving closer, he wrapped his arms around my waist and gently kissed my cheek and down my neck. I shivered as he led me by the hand to his bed.

He caressed me softly with his strong hands. I sighed as he slowly unbuttoned my blouse, kissing me tenderly. The first time was more awkward than a Harlequin novel. It was a mixture of hunger, and embarrassing awareness of my imperfections, but I gave in to my desire. His skin was pale, and there was a masculinity to him, bred from his work on the farm, and his career as a sheriff. I was not surprised. What aroused me was his confidence and delight in my pleasure. Our clothes littered the floor as we made love passionately. Later, he held me close while we talked about our future. I felt protected in his arms. Country music played softly on the radio. He told me which station was his favorite. "Listen to the words," he whispered, "they always tell a story." I became a fan.

We learned a lot about each other. He grew up in North Omaha. When he was a teen, he got a girl pregnant. He tried to look the child up once but hit a stone wall with the family. I told him about the schools I had attended. My unrestricted college days. My first serious love, who Mom didn't think was good enough. I wished she hadn't meddled. And yes, I'd ridden horses on trail rides as a child.

After an ardent good night kiss on my porch, I called Hal and John to let them know I was off the market. I had met someone, and we were getting serious. Each tried to convince me that he was a better choice but to no avail. My mind was made up.

Cooper invited me to Woodland's Annual Fire and Rescue Squad Banquet – a dinner sponsored by the county to honor the men and women who volunteer their time to save lives.

"It's our county's four-star event. You will be my showpiece. Everyone will want to know who's hanging on the sheriff's arm." He was a pillar of the community, after all.

Elated at being his eye-candy, I dressed to the nines in a long-sleeved maroon silk blouse, straight black skirt with a gold chain belt and black Italian pumps. Admiring myself in the mirror, I thought, "Cooper will be proud."

Before the banquet, we stopped to meet his mother, Nell, an attractive, vivacious woman in her mid-sixties. It had been many years since her divorce from Len, Cooper's father. Movie-star handsome, he liked to carouse, and it was difficult for her to trust him, given his track record of bar brawls and womanizing. Since the split, she had found God, came to peace with losing Len and made many friends. I would soon be one of them. Her short wavy brown hair had a sprinkling of gray at the temples. She was warm and had a delightful sense of humor. We hit it off. The three of us sat in her cluttered parlor where family images adorned the walls. There was a cute picture of Cooper in overalls when he was ten and Grant was eight with their grandparents, another photo of Grant dressed in full camouflage gear, gripping the antlers of a trophy buck, and one of Cooper missing a front tooth, holding a framed certificate he'd won for excellence in math. "Wow," I thought "rugged and smart." Hanging in the corner was a brass cage with a nervous and noisy parakeet. I was relieved that the two cats jumped on Nell's lap and not mine. She didn't match Cooper's description of the meddling mother.

I gushed about her son. "You must be so proud of Cooper."

She glanced toward the kitchen where he was pouring soft drinks, making sure he was out of hearing range then turned to me, lowered her voice, and said, "Cooper is different."

Three

Strolling arm in arm into the Fire Hall, I felt proud to be the illustrious county sheriff's date – a man larger and more intimidating than any man in the room. The town's people called him Bear for a reason. When I saw everyone's head turn in our direction, my confidence faltered. I wished they'd quit staring. *Is my belt twisted? My hair a mess?* We sat at a long, narrow table with Cooper's deputies and their wives. All emergency personnel were wearing their uniforms. I tried to join in conversations with the two women seated across from us, but they ignored me. Feeling very uncomfortable, I shifted in my seat. Did they perceive me as a city gal showing off, or could their standoffishness be attributed to my being a newcomer? I wasn't in their clique: I hadn't yet joined the sewing circle or stood in line behind them at the bank, the Post Office, or Pac A Sac. I didn't know their husbands, and our kids had never played in each other's yards. But nothing explained Cooper's sudden cold-shoulder. He didn't speak nor did he glance in my direction. His attention remained focused on the locals. When I tried to talk to him, he avoided eye contact as if I had two heads.

On our drive back to the city, I asked, "Why did you ignore me?"

His arm remained around my shoulder when he said, "That blouse doesn't look good on you. It makes you look old."

I flinched at the sting of his remark. "I spent a lot of time selecting this outfit."

"The color's wrong," he said impatiently.

Later, I hung the "old lady" blouse at the back of my closet to be sure I'd never wear it in his presence again, if at all. As we readied for bed, he thrust the knife blade deeper into my gut. "My mother thinks you're too old for me." I had no idea our eight-year age difference was an issue. Did she see me as a cougar?

When would Nell have made a comment? The entire time at her house, they were never alone. I said nothing.

The next morning, he held me close while we lay in bed. "Babe, I wake up every day and think of all the things I can see that you can't. I'm going to be your eyes". His words made me feel wrapped in a blanket of warmth. Cooper was again my compassionate, caring, loving protector. I forgave him for his cruel treatment at the banquet and his unkind words. But I would never forget.

"I love you," I said, snuggling closer.

When he broached the topic of our living together, I did not hesitate. He called one evening. "The county commissioners have given me permission to commute. We can live at your house or the farm." His voice broke. "The decision is yours." He began to cry with huge, gulping sobs.

His tears tugged at my heart. I would sacrifice metro living: sidewalks, bookstores, friends – for fresh air, wide-open spaces, and love. "We'll live on the farm," I said, anxious to please him.

His crying ceased as if a spigot had been turned off. "Babe, your home will be our weekend getaway. We'll have our choice of restaurants. We can shop at Hy-Vee on the way back to the country. Best of both worlds."

Margo kept track of my flowering relationship. Our habit was to talk three or four times a day. We chatted about everything from men to books to news headlines. Barely able to contain my excitement, I blurted, "I'm moving to the farm!"

She was aghast. "Have you thought this through? You've only known him six weeks."

How dare she question my decision? "At my age, I know what I want in a man."

"You're acting like a schoolgirl."

"Margo, I've never been so in love. Cooper's right for me. I wake up thinking about him and fall asleep dreaming of our exciting life together."

"Please don't leave me alone to swim with the sharks."

"I thought you'd be happy for me. Isn't this why we joined *The Hookup*?" Now that I had found a match, I was suddenly the selfish friend?

Margo and I had met several years earlier when I interviewed her for a book I was writing on widowhood. Our first husbands had died when we were in our thirties.

Our friendship grew through common interests. Each of us had remarried, were now divorced and had adult children, and were insatiable readers. Like the men we dated, we often exchanged our favorite titles. She is an intelligent drama queen, average height, slender, curly black hair with flecks of gray and dark brown eyes. Men are attracted to her spirited personality. Very domestic, she cooks, cleans, sews, and loves gardening. She was raised in the country, though looks and acts city-bred with an extensive vocabulary and urban style.

She was so depressed at the prospect of my moving that I urged Cooper to introduce her to one of his single friends. Then I would have my man and my confidante nearby. That was before I became familiar with the phrase, "Be careful what you wish for." Cooper enjoyed playing cupid and called his best friend, Michael Sutherland, and arranged dinner for the four of us in the city. Several days before the date, like Henry Higgins coaching Eliza Doolittle in *My Fair Lady*, Cooper prepped Margo on what she needed to do to meet Michael's requirements. "He's 6'5" and drawn to tall, willowy women. Wear stiletto heels. Show some leg. Surely you own a little black dress?"

She nodded.

"Perfect. Michael lives on coffee. Match him cup for cup."

After dinner, Margo was so wired she teetered on her heels. Michael was smitten. They began dating exclusively, making a winsome couple. Soon a For Sale sign appeared on her front lawn. She had questioned me for my impulsiveness, but her move to Woodland preceded mine.

I was thrilled and apprehensive about moving in with Coop. There would be little privacy. Would he tire of seeing me every day? Familiarity could breed conflict. It's strange to me now that I never thought that I might tire of him.

I waited until the last minute to pack. I couldn't bear another maroon blouse debacle. Cooper's only advice had been to bring long underwear and boots. Pulling my suitcase and cosmetic bag from the spare bedroom closet, I put in vials of makeup, perfume, and lingerie. That part was easy. When it was time to pack my clothes, I stood at my closet door and stared, paralyzed. Afraid of not looking pretty and sexy, for my man. I was incapable of making a simple decision. I tossed in thermal underwear, his favorite nightgown, and a pink terry robe then changed my mind and decided on a sexier robe. I was still debating when the doorbell rang.

Cooper arrived promptly at noon on a frigid February day to collect me and my terrier, Niki. I greeted him with a kiss and went back upstairs to finish primping and figure out what else to pack. I should have felt comfortable asking for his help but didn't want to appear needy of his love and approval. I could hear his boots pacing the tile floor in the foyer and quickly threw some clothes in my suitcase and pulled some hangers off the closet bar. A small mountain of garments remained on the bed.

"Hurry up, woman! I've got chores."

A chill ran down my spine. "I'll just be a minute."

I quickly applied lipstick. Too much. I removed it and started over. The more I hurried, the slower I became.

"Come on," he yelled again. I was not to challenge his obsession with punctuality. I should have thoroughly questioned my obsession with him.

He threw my luggage into the trunk and tossed my hanging clothes on top. His red-and-white German shorthair, Duchess, lumbered into the Lincoln and flopped onto the backseat. Niki scampered up beside her. I sat stiffly by the door, instead of nestled in the crook of Cooper's arm. I stewed over what I may have left behind. Did I pack my toothbrush? Is my blue sweater still on the bed? I searched for words to dispel his anger. A tiff wasn't the ideal way to start living together, but I never considered backing out.

He lit a cigarette. His nostrils flared, lips pressed tight. He snapped, "You knew I was coming; why weren't you ready?"

I took a deep breath. "I'm sorry, Cooper. I had trouble deciding what to pack. It won't happen again."

I was brought up believing that to be worthy of love I had to be flawless. That belief turned out to be a curse. I would do my best to be perfect so Cooper would never withhold his love. Every relationship has some problems, I rationalized. These spats were isolated incidents. I'd be more vigilant.

It had snowed six inches. Road crews had cleared the main streets, pushing piles of dirty snow to the curb. In silence, we drove what was now becoming a familiar stretch – the road home. The cedars and burr oaks looked like a Hallmark card with the sun beaming through ice glistening on the branches. The look on Cooper's face softened. Maybe his anger had dissipated. We turned onto Woodland's Main Street, drove past sleepy businesses: the bank, Hank's

Hardware, Barbara's Beauty Box, a meat locker, and the much-needed post office and quickly reached the long stretch of isolated road leading to his farm. We passed his snow-covered mailbox and turned left into the plowed lane. He parked close to the detached garage.

While he unloaded the suitcases, and Duchess followed Niki as she explored this vast new territory, I investigated my new surroundings in a more proprietary manner. The two-story, eighty-year-old white clapboard house with blue trim and a screened-in front porch, was dwarfed by 160 acres under sparkling white snow. Several snow-laden evergreens framed the house. Cows scavenged the corn stalks in the adjoining fields. Two horses had stalls in the old, weathered barn. An assortment of vehicles: a '65 Camaro, a Model T, and his motorcycle were in the garage. A tractor and a truck were parked outside.

As I climbed the back steps, the aroma of burning firewood was welcoming. I entered a mudroom which held a freezer and hooks for Cooper's chore clothes. Two pairs of boots sat on a mat close to the door. It led to the kitchen that had been painted white in contrast to the brown linoleum floor. I felt claustrophobic in his home. I was moving from 3500 to 1200 square feet and from five bathrooms to one. I would have lived in a tree house to be with Cooper. It was a bachelor's home. His idea of décor was weapons and animal heads. As I looked around, I noted there were no personal items. No family photos or snapshots of children or parents or grandparents. Instinct told me not to try to make changes; not a problem since I had no interest in interior decorating.

The dining room was the nerve center of the house. A wood stove built into the corner was the focal point.

"Always keep the fire stoked. I don't want to relight it," Cooper instructed in his sheriff's voice.

He fed it fragrant wood from fall to spring. The stove provided welcome warmth from the frigid air. Pops, hisses, and sighs of burning wood soothed the soul. Smoke wafting in cold air drifted across the property as a winter sun dived into the bare treetops. Unless the thermometer read below freezing, the living area was a hothouse. Perspiration soaked my clothing – until I removed layers. Guests kept their visits short.

Mounted on the wall to the left of the stove was the head of a trophy buck. The big, brown, lifeless eyes seemed to harbor an angry glint of reproach. Or was it a warning? A red and white checkered oilcloth covered the oak table, and four chairs fronted a bay window that looked out to the driveway and yard. We drank coffee, ate meals, and entertained Cooper's friends there. In his captain's chair, back to the wall, he could see penetrable areas. Even in his home, he would not allow anyone to catch him off guard. From this vantage point, he told tall tales while he cleaned his guns. He had a repertoire of "war stories" – ones that made him look good. He told them so often that soon I could recite them word for word. He relished a captive audience where he was the center of attention; sucking all the oxygen out of the room.

Straight ahead was a small parlor or living room – large enough to hold his console TV, an uncomfortable straight-back dining room chair for me, and his rocker, which looked like it came straight from a hunter's shack. He also had a fainting couch that he placed under the windows which looked out on the enclosed porch.

He showed me the favorites in his arsenal. Leading me to the bedroom, he pulled a pearl-handled Derringer out of his boot and placed it under his pillow. "I never leave the farm without this baby." I followed him down the hall. He pointed to a rifle positioned above the dining room archway.

"This was my grandpa's," he said affectionately. "He gave it to me and taught me how to shoot when I was ten."

Poised on a window ledge in the kitchen was .357 magnum. In the dining room, a claw-foot, oak gun cabinet with glass doors housed the rest of Cooper' artillery. "A man's man," I thought, smiling to myself. It didn't occur to me that showing off his gun collection might be a tactic to keep me in line. Guns have always terrified me. Here I felt secure knowing that they were for my protection.

"I'm a survivalist," Cooper bragged.

"What's that?"

"We're prepared to protect our own."

"Against what?"

"Those who would try to take away our God-given rights. We are self-sufficient and don't want the government telling us how to live."

"Oh, that would never happen. We live in the land of the free."

"The CIA keeps a file on everyone. Even you."

"Why would they care about me?"

"Your money."

"That's unnerving."

"In case of an attack Michael and Margo will move in and help guard the farm."

"I don't understand." He sounded paranoid.

Cooper chuckled, "You are naïve. No need to worry. You're safe with me."

He took my hand and led me carefully down the steep basement steps. He pulled the light chain. The bare bulb swung back and forth, rolling shadows.

"That looks like enough canned goods to feed an army."

"I estimate these provisions will last six months," he said proudly. He pointed out two shelves that contained boxes filled with ammo, blankets, a flashlight, first-aid kit, toilet paper, water, police scanner, and a battery-operated radio. A propane generator sat in the corner, with extra canisters of fuel in the back.

Extreme, but, after all, he is the sheriff - a 'survivalist.' He would know things I'm not privy to.

Back upstairs, he pointed to a narrow hall closet – much smaller than his – where he hung my dress clothes. The linen closet next to it had four shelves where I crammed my folded garments and toiletries. I didn't even have one dresser drawer. I felt like a temporary guest. The feeling would continue throughout my years at the farm, but afraid to rock the boat, I never let my annoyance rise to the surface. A musty odor of mothballs and mold emanated from the staircase. The rich mahogany throughout the interior had absorbed this dank smell.

As the weeks passed, the farm tested my lifelong fear of rodents. The cats were unable to control the mouse population. There were traps set in the dark corners of every room. One evening, knowing Cooper would be home for dinner break, I had lasagna in the oven. Suddenly I heard Niki jumping and snarling, her nails scratching the wood floor in the dining room. A brown blur, much smaller than Niki, darted toward the stove. I screamed and climbed onto the kitchen stool. Safety was my priority. Then the monster scurried out of sight, so I hurried into the bedroom and slammed the door. Safe. I dialed my daughter, Diane, who lived in a small town one hundred miles away, for a strategy consultation. She suggested I let in one of the cats.

"I can't let them in! They're too wild!"

She sympathized. "I wish I were there to get rid of the varmint for you."

A car door slammed.

"Never mind. I think Cooper's home."

I rushed into the kitchen, stepping carefully. I flung open the mudroom door; it slammed against the freezer. A young man was unloading the lawnmower he had repaired. "Paul, I need your help! Quick!"

He ran inside.

Pointing, I shrieked, "Get that creature out of here!"

He looked at the mouse with amusement. A crooked smile crept to his lips "Don't worry. It's a baby."

He snatched up the beast by its tail and tossed it in the yard. The cats batted it around for entertainment. When I saw Paul in town, we laughed about the incident.

This city woman was adapting to the rural lifestyle. When two newborn calves struggled for life in the cold, deep snow of February, Cooper zipped up his Carhartts, trudged out into the knee-deep, bitterly blowing snow, and gently carried the calves into the house. He set them tenderly on an old wool blanket in front of the wood stove and fed them three times a day from a large calf nursing bottle with milk from their mother. It was amazing to watch them fight for survival. Like magic, his care was healing. A man who loves nature must have a spiritual inclination. It didn't dawn on me until later that he was merely protecting his investment.

My initiation to country life was that glamorous. Cooper's routine remained the same. I was the one who struggled to adjust. Like Eva Gabor on *Green Acres,* I cooked and cleaned in silk blouses, designer jeans, full makeup, and boa slippers. The only thing I didn't do was climb a pole to use the telephone. I was determined to acquire the soul of a farmer.

Four

Cooper's truck rumbled up the gravel drive, triggering a Pavlovian response. I shifted to my role of the happy housewife, playing the part he expected to see when he arrived home. That behavior was a coping mechanism that I developed. By trying to perfect things on the outside, I could secure peace on the inside. The truth is, some days I wasn't in a good mood or up to the ridiculous task of faking cheerfulness. But as always, I greeted him at the door with a big smile.

He slipped his arm around my waist and pulled me against his firm chest, kissing me passionately. "I love coming home. You're always in a good mood."

He poured coffee and headed to the bedroom to change. As he passed the smoldering wood stove, he exploded. "What the hell? Why did you let the fire die out?"

"It's nice out. I didn't think I needed it in the springtime." I said, cowering from his anger.

He slammed his cup down; coffee splashed all over the table. I watched the dogs lower their heads and slink out of the room. I wanted to follow. Cooper grabbed kindling and matches and relit the fire.

"Woman, use your college-educated brain and open a damn window!" He yelled.

I cringed. "I'm sorry, Coop." I hated it when he screamed at me.

Why did I let the fire go out? Nobody perishes from a little sweat. Since my move to the farm, he had become increasingly critical and demanding. I was not to break any of his rules. He required my undivided attention. I gave it. Sex was a nightly expectation. We accomplished it. Personal phone calls must be kept to a minimum when he was home. Reading was permitted only in the parlor or dining room and never in bed as he insisted on complete darkness. My need for his approval was vital to my emotional well-being, so I concealed feelings that he might regard as negative and tried to never argue with him.

How I grew into a pushover goes back to my youth.

Aunt Sybil's eyes glittered with icy malevolence. "Look at you. Fifteen years old and you can't fasten a belt properly. Step over here."

I obeyed. My mother's older sister reached in front of her, yanked the belt, pulling me toward her to refasten it. I gripped the wall to brace myself. We were in the fitting room of an upscale Oklahoma City clothing store.

Mom said nothing. The saleswoman stared at the floor. I stood belted and humiliated. I blinked back tears. I hated the way my aunt treated me. I wanted to vaporize; evaporate; turn to dust – anything to be out of there.

Aunt Sybil snapped open her sterling silver cigarette case, took out two Pall Malls, and handed one to Mom. Her cheeks sucked in as she inhaled, looking over the red embers like a wicked crow. Shaking her head, she said. "You are lazy and selfish. You think of no one but yourself."

Later, I complained to Mom. "She makes me feel stupid and ugly. I don't like going anywhere with her. Why does she have to go with us?" Mom took Aunt Sybil's side, "She loves you. That's why she takes the time and trouble to correct you."

Thus, I began to associate control and criticism with love. Sometimes love hurts.

Most weekends, we went to my house in the city. Cooper enjoyed the change of pace. Although I looked forward to going home, I was always on edge during our weekly commutes. I worried that I'd forget something and have to bother Cooper to replace it. I dreaded hearing, "How the hell did you forget your makeup?" On Friday afternoons, after Cooper arrived home from work we loaded Niki and Duchess and our overnight bags into Cooper's classic, candy-apple red Camaro. At traffic lights, he revved the souped-up engine, showing off his toy. Car buffs gave a thumb's up. I rolled my eyes. His juvenile behavior may have been appropriate for a sophomore in high school, but not a sheriff.

When we reached my house, we climbed the steep driveway and parked in front of the two-car garage. Like a limo driver, Cooper opened the door for the pampered princesses. Niki pranced to the front door; Duchess waddled behind, both impatient for me to find the lock. Inside they settled on the leather couch in the living room.

During these weekends, Cooper was the urban cowboy, and I was the tour director. Weather permitting, we jumped on his motorcycle and headed to one of our favorite restaurants. Sometimes we'd go for a late-night ride. His badge was off. As he hoisted his leg over the leather seat, I fantasized that he was an outlaw and I was his babe perched behind. I loved knowing that people were watching us as we sped down the street.

We often crossed to the wrong side of the tracks: his old stomping grounds. The further northeast we cruised, the more menacing the neighborhoods. Thugs, drug dealers, and call girls eyed us from street corners. Ordinarily, I wouldn't be in that area after sunset, but with Cooper as my protector, I felt invincible. I tried not to think about what my mother would say.

He shouted over the wind and loud pipes. "Kids are playing outside, and it's after midnight."

I was indignant, "Where are their parents?"

"Papa's probably doing time and Mama's inside on her back scratching out a living."

"That's terrible."

"We're not all born with a silver spoon."

As much as Coop relished these getaways, he was most content when we returned to the farm on Sunday. His happiness made me euphoric, knowing that the odds were in my favor for a stress-free evening. Never as comfortable on concrete as with dirt under his boots, he lit a cigarette and the wood stove. Then he fed the animals and repaired a screen door or piece of machinery, while I put the groceries away and started dinner.

Life soared to dizzying heights when Cooper expanded my visual limitations. I appreciated him sharing experiences with me, he was patient. Early one warm spring evening as I was washing dishes, he rushed in and grabbed my soapy hand. "Quick, Babe, come outside." I put on my sunglasses, and he led me to the back stoop.

"Look!" he said, turning me to the west, and putting his arm around me. "There's a hot air balloon floating over the barn. Two people are standing in the basket."

"How exciting!" I shielded my eyes, squinting from the setting sun. "All I see is a gray blur."

"It's every color of the rainbow."

"It sounds beautiful. I wonder where they're going."

"Who knows? Just enjoy the view."

I squeezed his hand.

When we were out on the town, Cooper took great pains to camouflage my failing vision. With his arm around me, we waltzed into restaurants like Fred Astaire and Ginger Rogers. He understood more than anyone how embarrassed I felt when I stumbled and fell or accidentally bumped someone in the head with my purse or elbow.

In public, my eyes make me feel red in a room full of beige. Often, it's easier to stay home than worry about tripping over obstacles and colliding with people. The way others perceive my eyesight makes me self-conscious. Their comments have stung my ears too many times; "Watch where you're going, lady," or "Can't you see me sitting here?" Society tends to believe that someone with a physical challenge is also mentally challenged. Not true. When I complained to Diane, she said, "You're proving them wrong."

"Perhaps I'm too sensitive," I said to my friend.

"How can you not feel that way? It goes with your handicap. People would rather lose an arm or a leg. They fear the loss of vision more than any other catastrophe."

Contrary to the advice of my ophthalmologist, I had skipped my examination for three years. I dreaded the grueling exams; the burn when they dilated my pupils. Visual acuity using a standard eye chart, refraction and screening tests needed for R.P. patients. I would walk out with a tension headache. I finally quit procrastinating, and Margo drove me to the appointment. Leaving the doctor's office, I was ecstatic.

"Thank God there's no change in my eyesight. What a relief!"

"That's great news," Margo said, putting the key into the ignition.

I could hardly contain my excitement as we left the interstate and turned onto Highway 4. Now that my worries were alleviated, I could enjoy the beauty of the countryside. The smells of spring were fresh and invigorating. We drove through rolling hills of heavily wooded terrain, interspersed with a patchwork of newly planted fields and pastures. Everything was coming to life. The bright green buds of the oak, maple, and cottonwood trees were beginning to open.

When Margo dropped me off at the farm, I couldn't wait to share my good news with Cooper. He and several of his buddies were cutting firewood. He threw his axe into the stump and strolled over to greet me.

"Cooper," I burst out, "the doctor said my R.P. is in remission!"

Coop stared at me. "He doesn't live with you." His words cut through me like a dull, jagged knife. I had expected him to say, "That's terrific! Let's celebrate." Instead, he returned to his friends and his wood pile. I was growing wary of Cooper's mood swings, but this was different. He hostile, and he meant to hurt me. It was true my vision wasn't as sharp as it used to be. But he didn't have to say it like that. I hurried up the crooked back steps – side stepping a gray kitten snoozing in the warm sunshine. Not wanting Cooper to see my tears, I ran to the bedroom, collapsed on the bed, and sobbed until I felt drained. By the time dinner was served, he'd forgotten his vicious words. Expecting me to do the same, he was back to his boisterous self. I would never forget them.

Later that evening I met his brother Grant. The three of us sat in the dining room at the farm and had a friendly visit. While sipping soft drinks, the brothers reminisced. Suddenly Cooper said that they were going outside for a while. They'd be right back. It was the first time he had excluded me. I watched them as they sat on the picnic table deep in conversation, thinking to myself, *something's not right. What's the big secret?* Instinct told me that Cooper had explained to Grant, "I'm living with her because she's loaded and going blind. Just wait, her fortune will be in my bank account." But I didn't want to lose him, and I ignored my discomfort.

Weeks later Cooper strolled into the kitchen whistling. In his hands was a nice, large green head of lettuce from his garden.

"Look at this, Babe!" He held it out at arm's length. "It could be on the cover of *Organic Gardening.*"

As I put the lettuce in the sink to soak, an insect crawled up my arm. I screamed. "Get this bug off me!"

He scooped it up and threw the pest out the back door.

I started to throw the lettuce in the trash can.

He yanked it from my hand yelling, "What the hell are you doing? You don't toss fresh vegetables out just because of a harmless beetle. When I was on shift yesterday, a gypsy family was scavenging for food in garbage cans behind Pac A Sac. They know what it's like to be hungry! Damn spoiled city woman." He rinsed the lettuce and put it in the fridge; water dripped on the lower shelves.

Grabbing a pack of cigarettes, he bolted out the back door. Afraid he would leave for good, I followed him to the stoop. "Where are you going?"

No answer. Just the sound of his boots tromping down the steps.

"Cooper, please come back. I'm sorry."

He disappeared into a thick grove of trees bordering the pasture. This pattern of behavior had become agonizingly familiar. I never dared ask where he went. Did he have a hidden survivalist bunker out in the woods? Stocked with more guns, ammo, and supplies?

As I dragged myself back into the house, I felt depressed and guilty – hating myself for my childish behavior. He always managed to project the blame onto me. Niki offered a warm, wet nose as she and Duchess consoled me. "I've done it this time," I thought. "If he doesn't dump me at my house, I'll get the silent treatment. I hate it when he acts like I'm not here and refuses to talk to me."

Thank God for the phone. My friends were only eleven digits away. Since I paid the bill and only made calls when Cooper was gone, he didn't complain. I rang California, praying Sara, the life coach, was not with a client. While living in Omaha, she facilitated a women's support group that I attended at the University of Omaha. We'd meet once a month at the members' homes for an hour of socializing and much-needed venting.

She picked up. "Cooper and I had another fight. He's terribly angry."

She sighed, probably thinking, "Here we go again." "About what?"

"I freaked over a bug in the lettuce and tried to throw it away. He blew up and is hiding somewhere on the farm."

"Good, maybe he'll fall in a hole and never come back." I didn't say anything. "How much longer are you going to put up with him?"

"You don't understand Sara. It's all my fault."

"If you're dead set on staying, stand up for yourself!"

"I need to go, I hear him at the back door."

I wiped my eyes and greeted him with a hug and an apology. Darkness had fallen. He didn't say a word but grabbed an afghan off the couch in the parlor. Taking my hand, he guided me to the picnic table. I laid back not caring that the hardwood pressed into my shoulder blades. A silvery moon loomed behind the clouds. He whispered, "I love you more than life."

As the breeze caressed our skin, we made love – wildly, hungrily. Gazing at the countless stars in the night sky, I was elated and dismissed the disappearing acts, temper tantrums, and harsh words. He was an emotionally unrestrained guy. Fighting didn't seem so bad when you made up with such passion.

Five

Cooper shoved the flutter-wheeled cart directly to the meat counter where every possible prime cut of beef, pork, poultry, lamb, and an assortment of bratwurst and seafood lay spread before us like an exotic buffet. He selected his favorite, a half-dozen thick New York strip steaks. Why couldn't he ever pick my preference – the wild Alaskan pink salmon filets? He was not bashful about living large at my expense. He and the butcher were on a first name basis.

If we shopped in the city, it was my responsibility, "Babe, you go ahead and take care of this, and I'll buy at Pac A Sac." To me, it made sense. Of course, in time the only thing we'd purchase in Woodland would be a loaf of bread, a box of cereal or an occasional pound of ground chuck or butter with the coupon from the local Pac A Sac ad.

As time passed, our grocery bill resembled an insurance co-pay. I paid eighty, and he paid twenty. I grew increasingly resentful but swallowed my feelings, telling myself that it seemed petty for a couple who was so in love to argue over grocery store receipts.

The only expenditures Cooper didn't renege on were those we ate meals out. One evening we finished dinner at the Pink Poodle, a tiny, unassuming restaurant located on an old back highway that packed in customers for their famous prime rib. It was my turn to treat. To preserve his pride, I slipped him my credit card. He had become proficient with my signature and signed my name with a flourish. I couldn't have done it better myself.

Putting his arm around me, he said, "Thanks, Babe, that king size cut did the trick."

When we dined at Piccolo Pete's the next evening, Cooper pulled out his billfold, flashing a thick wad of bills. "Thank you, honey," I said, "My filet was perfect." I smiled as we locked arms to cross the parking lot.

On Cooper's forty-fourth birthday, I beamed as he slipped on the tailored black leather jacket I had lovingly purchased. When I spotted the coat in Berman's Leather Wear, I knew it would make the ideal gift – a 'Live to Ride' and 'Ride to Live' sentiment that enhanced his tough guy persona. It was something personal that no one else would have thought to buy him.

He preened like a peacock, turning left and right, grinning at himself in the mirror. The fit was perfect, the style classy. Sam Elliott couldn't look as ruggedly handsome. A wonderful, warm feeling washed over me. I loved making Cooper happy.

His mother had joined us at the farm for the celebration. Her gift was a jar of freshly canned peach jam. She shook her head. "You're spoiling him." I didn't catch her hidden message. *"Careful. He sees dollar signs when he looks at you."* Her subtle warning went over my head.

Nell and I could talk about anything, and we often did. Except for her son. And when she spoke of him, it was snippets of his youth and the reality of his adulthood. I heard a lot of contradictory remarks to some of the tales he had woven. I never questioned his integrity, though, wanting only to see the good.

Coop's gifts to me were predictably a chrysanthemum plant or fresh flowers purchased from Pete at *Petals* and a sentimental card with syrupy words penned under the verse: "Babe, I will love you always," or "I can't live without you." Flowers were nice, but I would have appreciated a book or something from the heart occasionally.

At Margo's urging, Michael decided to sell his Honda Gold Wing to pay off some of his debts. When we went to their house to test drive the bike, Margo was sitting in the driveway on a stepstool with a cigarette in one hand and a cup of coffee in the other. Michael, in a dirty t-shirt, was working on a vintage '58 Ford; a cigarette dangled from the corner of his mouth. Looking up, he skinned a knuckle on a stubborn engine mount. He cursed and sucked at the torn flesh. "Bear, it never fails." He threw a greasy rag on his toolbox. "Take the scoot out while I'm feeling too accident-prone to keep it. The keys are in it."

Cooper jumped on the bike. "Come on woman, let's ride."

I put on my black rebel scarf and sunglasses and climbed behind. As we sped past the police station, Sweet Shoppe, and grocery store, he enjoyed the throaty sound of a well-tuned engine. I basked in the stares of onlookers. On a hillside, we stopped at a gravel turnout to watch the sunset. It was beauty at its best, a panorama of green trees and pink marbled clouds etched in gold.

"Glorious," I said, squinting into the setting sun. There's nothing better than intimacy in a place of natural beauty.

"We'll each pay half," he told me, wiping the gas tank with his handkerchief.

"What about the motorcycle you've been riding?"

"I'll sell it. It's pushing twenty years. This one's only two. It's a lot safer."

I nodded, careful to conceal my anger. I didn't even own a car anymore. Why would I buy an even greater liability risk?

"Babe, we'll raise hell." He revved the throttle to juice my adrenaline, "Fifty/fifty?"

"Fifty/fifty," I said, forcing a smile.

The sun was fading behind Venetian blind clouds. Cold air crept out of the trees to sting my flesh. I couldn't tell him no. Mainly because I was terrified he'd leave but also because of his red-hot temper. We returned to Michael's the following day with the money. The motorcycle was "ours." Properly spelled: H.I.S.

Through police work, Cooper was privy to questionable people and opportunities. I was in denial and refused to believe that he could be a bad cop. After all, one doesn't climb the ladder to success without being reputable, especially in law enforcement. Ruthlessness was one thing. Craftiness tipped the balance in any number of elections. Using the badge to further criminal activity seemed below him.

Life with Cooper was an ongoing adventure. He derived pleasure by shocking me. We could be enjoying chicken cordon bleu at the French Café or eating barbecued ribs with bikers at Doc's.

One afternoon he said, "I've got an appointment. Come with me." On the drive, Cooper coached me on what to expect at Doc's. "The house is a revolving door of tattooed characters. Connie and her old man, Stone, are cokeheads. She's got two rug-rats fathered by God knows who. Chainsaw, the club mechanic, is a confirmed bachelor. He's using junkyard parts to rebuild a '69 pan-head in the dining room."

I gasped. "There's a motorcycle where they eat?" Where was he taking me? A house or a garage?

"Duh, if it were outside, it would be stolen. Chainsaw takes payment in cash or drugs. Doc's old lady Debbie is the club mama. She's large and in charge. She polices the kids, makes sure her old man's stomach is full and keeps the cold beers coming."

We parked in the driveway of a small one-story house and walked around to the back along a cracked and narrow sidewalk, pushing branches from an overgrown bush out of our way. A heavily chained pit bull guarded the front. What was I doing here? I sat on a folding chair in the dining room, feeling overdressed and out of place, while Coop conducted his *business* with Doc. I looked around wide-eyed, clutching my Coach bag closer to my body. The bike frame stood on top of a blue plastic tarp. Motorcycle parts, open tool boxes, and grease rags were scattered everywhere: a set of wrenches on an end table, dirty tires leaning against a wall. For me, brought up with silk curtains and lampshades, and linen napkins with matching tablecloths, it was jaw dropping. Chainsaw was a big guy with a goatee, hands coated with grease up to his elbows, wearing a muscle shirt. He never once looked up as he tinkered on his chopper.

A young woman sat down cross-legged on the floor beside me and babbled endlessly. She bounced from one subject to another. I had trouble following her conversation.

As we drove away, I asked, "Why did you leave me alone with Chatty Cathy? She talked non-stop."

Cooper lowered his eyebrows, "What did she talk about?"

"I don't have a clue. She just rambled on."

He shook his head, "Her brain is fried."

We sped toward home at getaway speed. I was unconcerned. "After all, he's the sheriff," I thought proudly. With fence posts whipping by on one side and traffic on the other, it was like competing in a drag race. We whizzed by silos, barns, and billboards. The overcast sky deposited a brooding gray patina upon the countryside.

"The house had a funny smell," I said.

He shot me a cold glance. "If the county wanted me to have a drug dog, they would have issued one. Doc's a snitch, and I needed information. Stay out of police business and keep your mouth shut."

"Mum's the word." I moved closer to him.

He pressed his thigh against mine. Sexual heat. Who could ask for better reassurance?

One afternoon as I was reading, Coop rushed in the back door. "Let's go, Babe!"

"Where to?"

"It's a surprise."

I put my book and magnifier on the dining room table and followed him to his Lincoln, parked in the drive, thinking he was taking me out for an ice cream treat. We drove an hour down the road to Rolling Meadows Trailer Park; located in the middle of a heavily wooded area. He parked in front of a weathered singlewide. The tiny yard was overgrown with a formidable patch of nettles.

He walked over to my side of the car. "Sit tight. Roll your window up and lock the door. I'll be right back."

Who are we now, Bonnie and Clyde? I waited a bit nervously, unable to hop behind the wheel and speed away. I looked at the residence and its neighbors. All were in various stages of neglect. Coop emerged ten minutes later and climbed into the car. "Here's the deal. Gus is hurting for money. He's got a hot twelve-gauge shotgun. It cost him $2,500. I can buy it for a thousand. It's a steal. How about an early Christmas present?"

The last thing Cooper needed was another firearm. A Charles Manson look-alike opened the sagging trailer door. His appearance was well timed. I shuddered. "Let's go."

I didn't want to buy the damn gun any more than I wanted to buy the damn motorcycle. Cooper had the resources to enlarge his arsenal but chose to spend my money so he could save his. He relished living the high-life. I was getting tired of being his banker and becoming disgusted by his endless greed: his lust for possessions. But I buckled to hold on to his love. We headed to town. I entered the bank alone and withdrew the cash. I wasn't at the place where NO had the nerve to leap from my usually bitten tongue.

In Cooper's world, true love meant opening my billfold, forgetting that the broad road to bankruptcy and homelessness is too much indulgence and avoidance of the simple little word NO. I had never learned to stand up for myself.

Six

"Mom, I think you should consider buying shares of Berkshire Hathaway. Warren Buffett is C.E.O. Argus lists it as a strong buy."

It was Mark calling from New York where he had recently gotten a position as a stock analyst. After studying the market since his teens, he had a pretty good sense of what would be profitable. Investing was the only profession that he had ever set his sights on. He also had a strong conviction of not handing out free advice to family members, but he truly believed and trusted this investment.

Cooper, hovering nearby so he could listen in on our conversation, looked at me expectantly, ready to jump on the bandwagon.

I turned my back to him and lowered my voice. "Thanks, Mark, I'll think about it and call you tomorrow," then I cut the long line to New York.

Cooper paced the kitchen, hands in his pockets. "What's wrong with you, woman? Has your hair bleach polluted your brain? Why didn't you listen to Mark? He eats, breathes, and sleeps investments. If it were me, I'd be on the phone with my broker now."

"But, it's not you," I thought, refilling my coffee to avoid his menacing gaze. So, if you want to buy, use your money and get your broker. What did Cooper know about investing? How could he tell me what risks to take when he didn't know the market? My intention was to have ONE boundary. I would buy him things. But my investments were MY investments! No Berkshire Hathaway! I would not give in this time! To prove my point, I ignored the best free investment advice I ever received. I sabotaged my future earning power by not calling my financial advisor.

Coop grabbed his coffee and stormed out of the room. He didn't speak to me the rest of the day.

Months later, in the city, on a sun-blessed Saturday morning, vivid roses bloomed on the vines in my yard. I patiently waited for Cooper. We were going to the Pancake House for breakfast. My mouth watered as I anticipated pancakes smothered in maple syrup. Mark, home for the Fourth of July weekend, was upstairs sleeping. Suddenly the garage door slammed. Cooper stormed into the kitchen. Niki and Duchess retreated to the couch, tails tucked between their legs.

"Your son, the child prodigy, siphoned gas out of my Camaro."

Oh, get real, I thought. "Why would Mark do that?"

"You tell me. He's your kid. He probably wanted to piss me off or start trouble between you and me."

Mark already knew there was no shortage of angst in my situation. He would not purposely set out to aggravate the relationship.

"Mark's beyond childish pranks," I said. "Besides, the smell of gas makes him sick." As a boy, his reaction to gasoline fumes was so severe that he could not fill the lawn mower.

Coop hissed, "I'm telling you that's what happened. Let's go."

As we backed down the driveway, I thought about his ridiculous accusation. Could Cooper be right? Did he see something in Mark that I hadn't spotted in twenty-seven years of motherhood?

Cooper was rough around the edges but there were redeeming moments, like the day Diane had to drive to Des Moines on business. He said her car wasn't safe and offered his pickup for the trip. She was relieved to get reliable wheels. I was delighted he cared enough to help her.

"That is so thoughtful. Not being a driver anymore, I don't notice those things," I said.

"Most women don't."

He called in a favor. A mechanic friend made repairs while she was gone. Cooper was racking up points.

Then the day came when Diane needed a ride to the emergency room. She worked at the mall and had thrown her back out working long days in high heels behind a makeup counter.

"Her back! Did she blow a disc hustling lipstick? Bullshit!" Cooper snapped.

I went to her defense. "She lifts heavy boxes wearing three-inch heels." That was not apt to go over well; he was already red-eyed with fury. I wanted to make a comment about his back ailments, but it was not a good time for logic. It rarely was. Courts of law, after all, accepted his viewpoints.

"Kids" he snarled. He showed his disapproval by driving aggressively through traffic. He made the turn sharply into Emergency, and I slid into the door. Cooper dropped us at the entrance, leaving an aide to help her into a wheelchair. He was a strapping young man who gave a pretty woman special attention. After parking the car, Cooper begrudgingly joined us in the waiting area, which looked like an airport in a snowstorm. In one corner, a young woman kept checking her watch while eating a candy bar. A middle-aged man's cough sounded like a barking seal. The gangly woman sitting alongside him offered a wad of tissues from her purse. A family with three tired toddlers, one with a sagging diaper, made me glad my children weren't small anymore.

Cooper grumbled. He crossed and re-crossed his legs. "For crying out loud, there's not a damn thing wrong with you, Diane. Hell, I had a broken back. You don't hear me whining."

Heading for the coffee machine, he barked over his shoulder, "All you need is some rest. You'll be fine." People frowned. I was embarrassed. This physically imposing man had not a speck of empathy.

"He's making everybody miserable," Diane said.

"Nothing new," I thought, unable to excuse his insensitivity. There was enough evidence for any jury to convict him of being a quintessential jerk.

Cooper was in no better spirits when he returned with his coffee, steam rising from the Styrofoam cup. "I'm the one suffering. Because of this unnecessary ER trip, I missed dinner."

"Maybe the cafeteria is still open," I said, wishing he would shut up.

He strode outside to smoke.

"If we're lucky, an ambulance will run over him," Diane said. "I'll take a cab home."

Crunch time, stand by my daughter or side with my husband. "I'm not leaving you."

Mercifully, the nurse called Diane's name. The doctor diagnosed a problem with her sciatic nerve. He gave her a shot of Demerol and prescribed pain medication. After stopping at the pharmacy, I helped her get settled in her apartment. Cooper waited impatiently, not lifting a finger. At my house, the acrimony escalated. "I can't believe you didn't see through her act. Diane's faking and looking for sympathy."

Cooper was unusually perceptive about people. Was Diane manipulating me? If she was, why? My daughter was not the type to waste her time trying to enlist sympathy.

"It's nothing compared to what I've endured." Here we go again. All injuries paled in comparison to his. If he missed a day of work because of his back pain, he'd lie in bed and whine, expecting me to wait on him hand and foot. It was always about Coop. He could turn a shipwreck in the Baltic into something about him.

Cooper's anger manifested itself in dead silence. He emphasized his viewpoint by withholding affection. No touching, no pillow talk. He spent the night on the couch in the family room – the room furthest from the bedroom. The next morning the alluring aroma of bacon, eggs, toast, and coffee mellowed him. We didn't speak a word about the previous evening and were once again a loving couple.

Cooper left to buy cigarettes. I called Diane to be sure she was on the mend.

"I'll live," she said. "Can you say as much?"

Gail wasn't a problem for him because she lived in Texas. She wrote columns for popular magazines. His only problem with her was our lengthy phone conversations which took my attention away from him. He made sarcastic remarks during and after our calls. I finally told her, "Call me between his regular shift hours, unless it's an emergency."

At times, the whole family felt that we'd been indicted and booked in his maximum-security jail.

Seven

One spring morning after a brisk walk and a peaceful start to my day, the next thing I remember is Cooper yelling, "Pack your bags! I'm taking you home!" He stormed outside, slamming the door behind him so hard the windows rattled.

He was discarding me like damaged goods. For what I can't remember.

I stood at the kitchen window, suitcase at my side, body trembling, tears streaming down my face. *What did I do?* I watched as he drove his John Deere back and forth tilling the soil, knowing better than to go out to try to talk to him. He planted rows of lettuce, radishes, and green onions seeds that we had previously purchased from Hank's Hardware. He dug holes and dropped in cucumber seeds, then refilled the holes carefully, building mounds of dirt, and dusting his hands on his jeans. Finally, he put in the pepper and tomato plants, then spent another thirty minutes watering the area. When he finished, he picked up a stick to wipe the mud from the sole of his boots. I prayed that his rage had dissipated; that he'd walk through the door and enfold me in his arms and say, 'I love you. You're not going anywhere.'

Four hours later he trudged up the back steps and said, "We're leaving." My heart sank as he grabbed my suitcase, walked out the door, and threw it in the trunk. My mind raced: how can I make this right? But it was already set in motion.

I made my way to the car, struggling to see through tears, forcing my feet to move. Niki ran ahead and jumped in the back seat. I sat close to the door, apologizing for unknown transgressions all the way home. I must have done something wrong. He'd never hurt me like this. He stared at the isolated country road in ominous silence.

By the time we pulled into the driveway, my throat felt raw, and my eyes were swollen from hours of crying; mascara smeared my face. Alarmed that this was the last time I'd see him, I pleaded, "Cooper, you know how much I love you. Please don't leave me."

Without speaking, he yanked my suitcase from the trunk and tossed it on the front porch. It hit the door with a loud *thump*. Still sobbing, I stepped out of the car. He roared away, leaving me standing on my stoop with the stench of burnt rubber in the air.

Niki was jubilant as we entered the house, happy to be home. Me? I just knew I'd never see him again.

Several hours later Margo arrived, with a warm shoulder and a head cold. Kleenex filled the wastebasket as I bawled and she blew her nose and sneezed germs everywhere. Not once did I consider the hours of anguish Cooper put me through waiting at the window while he tilled his garden. I finally fell asleep in the early morning hours, only to awaken a short time later and resume the self-torture all over again. Why did I always blame myself and never anyone else? I accepted whatever punishments he dealt me: whether it was his silent treatment or taking me home. I stopped trying to reason with him, fearing it would drive him further away.

Cooper shocked me by calling the next evening at midnight. His voice trembled, "I'm torn up and sick to my stomach. Why didn't you call?"

"I thought you never wanted to see or hear from me again."

"I can't live without you," he moaned.

Relief flowed through me. Cooper had forgiven me. But for what?

I ignored my Cousin Stephanie's advice. "If you're going back, lay down ground rules."

Rules? Right. I would have a better chance reading the bottom line of an eye chart. I didn't hesitate to board the roller coaster for another spin. Cooper's renewed expressions of love were a drug. The thrill of making up drove caution from my head like sunlight melting winter snow. It didn't matter why he acted so irrationally. All that mattered was that he wanted me back.

The next day Kira, a University student who lived in my basement apartment, drove me to the farm. I let myself in. When Cooper returned from work, he was overjoyed to see me. We made love, and all was forgiven. Once again, I reasoned that the good times more than compensated for the bad. A lover's quarrel tries one's nerves, but it's no match for making up.

Living with Cooper was an adventure for a woman who had always lived a sheltered life. One day I was Motorcycle Momma, holding on for dear life as we sped down a country road, the next Franny Farmer listening to titillating stories from the cop shop, or we were the odd couple at synagogue holding hands on High Holy Days.

Cooper came home from work two days later, and said, "Shorty asked when we're getting married."

That was my proposal.

Eight

My proposal wasn't as spine-tingling as having it illuminated on a billboard high above Highway 4. Nevertheless, I was so thrilled at the prospect of becoming Cooper's wife that his lack of sentiment and creativity didn't faze me. Nor did I give a thought to my recent banishment from the farm. I was wildly in love, and nothing could stop me from marrying the man of my dreams.

I thought of my prior marriages...

Barely twenty-one, I had only known Bruce (Boots) five months when we became engaged. This impetuous and illogical union was the next step in my life plan.

I had been pursued by numerous eligibles, but with little self-knowledge and no goals other than becoming a wife and homemaker – modeled after my mother – I was like a spinning top and Boots was where I stopped. I said yes, not because I loved him, but because I didn't know what else to do, and that's what all my friends were doing. Plus, he would be a good provider. As a partner in his father's insurance agency, Boots' future was bright.

Quiet and unassuming, he was someone you would overlook in a crowd. Tall, with thinning dark brown hair and kind brown eyes, at twenty-seven Boots was an old soul. All of this masked an intense nature in one never without a cigarette.

The week of the wedding, I felt confused and sick with doubt. Without knowing who I was, making decisions about a life partner was a bad idea. One day while sitting at my parent's grand piano, I contemplated breaking off the engagement, but what would people say? With gowns purchased, the food ordered, and out of town relatives already arriving, the ceremony went on as scheduled. Before we started a family, I wish I'd had the guts to say, "You're a wonderful man, but we're mismatched." Sex was important to me; not him. We were intimate only if I initiated it. Perhaps things would have turned out differently if we had slept together before marriage, but that was taboo at the time.

At twenty-four I became pregnant with Gail. I was too immature for motherhood. For the last four months, I threatened to miscarry and was put on bed rest. Born thirty days premature, she cried for eight months, totally exhausting me. I went through major post-partum depression and had a hard time bonding with her. Two years later our son Mark was born. He was a contented baby, and I was not the high-strung mother I had been the first time around. When Gail was a toddler, she was diagnosed with R.P. and reminded me too much of someone I disliked. ME.

When she was twenty, she confronted me about the pain in our relationship. "You never loved me."

"Gail, you were always loveable. That was my fault. I couldn't love you until I learned to love myself."

When Mark was a healthy, mischievous, sloppy eight-year-old, not wanting to risk bringing another child into the world with an eye disease, Boots and I began the adoption process. We felt blessed when we adopted Diane.

When a major or minor crisis arose, I was on the phone to Boots' office. He was one of the kindest, sweetest men I have ever met, treating the children and me, his parents, as well as my mother, with love and respect. He was a devoted, hardworking husband. He had more patience with me than my parents. We had three energetic kids, whom we loved deeply, and money in the bank. Sixteen years after we married, he died of a heart attack. The children and I were devastated.

On Labor Day, a year after Boots' death, friends with match-making ideas invited the children and me to be their dinner guests at the country club. As we finished dessert, Donald and his two daughters Marjorie, twelve, and Abby, six, approached. His son Stuart, eighteen, had just joined the Navy. With leathery olive skin and a prominent nose, Donald looked Greek, was medium height, had an athletic build and wore Harry Potter spectacles. No fireworks, but since no one was knocking down my door, I turned on the charm.

He called two weeks later.

Donald was a medical school professor, with a military academy background, and saw everything in black and white.

As a child, he feared that his gambling mother would bet their home, so he learned to pinch pennies. An animal in the bedroom, he pursued with ardor. I was ambivalent — the minute he was enamored, I wanted space. But when he backed off, I looked for commitment. Even as my son walked me down the aisle a year later, I was still questioning my decision to marry the professor. In my naïveté, I gave little consideration to the pressures of blending two families, particularly with three teenagers.

His house was too small, and his pride wouldn't allow him to move into a house where the shadow of my former husband existed. I put my treasured home on the market and made the down payment on a two-story Cape Cod. One of my biggest regrets is leaving the ranch house on Sunset Trail; the home that I equated with security and serenity.

Our new home was filled immediately with tension. We were more like the Osbourne's than the Brady Bunch. Due to Donald's childhood scars, I functioned as a single parent. The pressure was preferable to him storming out the door or getting depressed every time the children misbehaved. My daily complaints about their behavior didn't help.

Two teenagers had to share a bedroom: my Gail, the studious nerd and his pot-smoking runaway, Marjorie. Above the garage in his own cave, one would think my teenage son Mark wouldn't have added misery. I finally gave up the battle against his sloppiness when I heard the cleaning woman barreling down the stairs screaming, "You can't pay me enough to walk into that room." He had booby-trapped his room with firecrackers.

It never got any better. Soon the six children bombarded us with drinking, smoking, frequent hospitalizations, bedwetting, running away, fist fights at school, truancy, stealing, collection agencies, teenage pregnancy, and a locked treatment facility. The only disaster I didn't encounter was head lice.

Forget about holding hands and sweet talk over wine. When Donald was home, he sat at the desk in the family room writing a book on bird anatomy.

When the four eldest children moved on, two high-schoolers remained. Just as things should have been settling down, Donald had an affair with an ambitious medical student. I chose to ignore it. The prospect of being alone seemed worse than the humiliation of playing second fiddle.

One evening Diane, now fifteen, was talking on the kitchen phone. Hearing her stepfather return from an evening jog, she quickly hung up. She was grounded from the phone and didn't want her punishment extended. I was in the basement writing a book on widowhood. Donald removed his muddy shoes and went upstairs. Figuring he was going to shower and she had more phone time, Diane picked up and heard a woman's voice.

"I love you, honey. See you tomorrow."

Donald blew a kiss into the phone, "I love you, Kitten."

Diane shouted, "Dad, you're sick!"

Kitten slammed down the phone.

Donald did too.

As he was running down the stairs two at a time, Diane screamed for me. I rushed up the stairs. "What's going on?"

Donald was in the kitchen, face sweaty, though not from running.

"Tell her! Tell her you're having an affair!"

Donald said, "I don't have to justify anything to you."

"Mom, make him leave. You and I will be fine. I'm getting my driver's permit. You don't need him."

"Drop it and go to bed. This is something Dad and I must discuss."

When she was out of earshot, I yelled, "Now you've done it, you jerk! She's a teenage time bomb, and she trusted you."

Diane felt betrayed by both of us; Donald for the infidelity and me for not standing up for myself.

One morning, months later I sat in bed reading The Bigamist's Daughter. Donald was thumbing through the latest issue of Bon Appétit.

I said, "Why don't you kiss me anymore?" He put his magazine down and dropped the bomb. "I want a divorce."

"How dare you leave me after I've raised your children for the last twelve years?"

He shrugged. "It's over."

The time came for us to divide property. We sat at the table with pencil and paper.

"Let's just split the house down the middle," he proposed.

"I made the down payment and monthly installments. Your only contribution was the minimal proceeds from your house."

"Now wait a minute," Donald argued. "I've spent every weekend since we married making improvements. I've painted, papered, laid carpet and repaired these chairs we're sitting on."

"You did all that because you were too cheap to hire help or buy new!"

I felt torn between fighting for what was rightfully mine and my fear of alienating him further and being left alone. I agreed to sell the house and split the proceeds. My attorney supported my decision.

The following Saturday my friend and I went to lunch. We hashed over details of the divorce. Suddenly I blurted, "I don't want to sell the house."

"Then don't."

Just what I needed to hear.

That evening I confronted Donald, "This is my home. I'm staying. You're the one that has to leave."

"I've slaved for this house!" He was furious.

"I've slaved for this marriage. I'm not leaving." I replaced my lawyer with a ruthless divorce attorney.

Donald moved out with his Wolfgang Puck pots and pans, stacks of Bon Appétit, and Grecian Formula. Single again, my heart was not broken, but my fear of being alone unnerved me.

Nine

My financial advisor, Evan Barnhill, President and CEO of Barnhill Investment Counsel, gave me a man's handshake, crushing my rings into my fingers. He looked distinguished, as did everyone in the office. Behind the times, he would frown if the women on his staff wore slacks. Taking my elbow, he guided me to his small office. It contained the usual clutter of financial research from brokerage firms, periodicals, and wall-to-wall family photos. "Make yourself comfortable," he said, pointing to a chair. "Dr. Pepper?" He knows me well.

"No thanks," I said sitting down facing him. Ostensibly, I was here for the semi-annual review of my portfolio. The truth was I was bursting to share my good news.

Evan took his place behind the old-style banker's desk. On the corner lay the morning issue of the *Wall Street Journal* folded in half. Post-it notes were stuck on it for later research. To his right was a well-worn cardboard box, once used by his father to store checks and deposit slips, proof of Evan's sentimental nature. When his executive staff moved into their spacious, professionally designed offices, Evan remained in his original 12x12. As CEO, he's entitled to front row parking but chooses to use space provided for employees. Keeping clients' money wisely invested is his bottom line. He says it's a humbling business. Although maintaining an unassuming façade, he is impressed nonetheless by the status of his well-heeled clients.

His lined face sported a boyish grin. Tall and lanky, he is round-shouldered from decades of lugging home a briefcase stuffed with responsibility each evening.

He put on his wire-rimmed glasses and opened my file. Because of Evan's enjoyment of the money game and having an eye for knowing where to spend your currency well, I am confident that my financial evaluation will be on the plus side. I respect his integrity and dedication to his clients and employees – who are hand-picked and treated like family. It has been a profitable alliance for both of us. Rubbing his chin, he said, "Your portfolio is shaping up nicely. We're showing an eight percent gain."

I waited for the right moment to interrupt.

He droned on. "The economy is strong. We'll buy stocks, not bonds."

The phone jangled.

"Excuse me; I must take this call."

I tapped my foot impatiently. I tolerate the intrusions because Evan has the Midas touch.

Replacing the receiver, he said, "The election is not far off. We don't know if taxes will go up. It depends on whether Reagan wins re-election. The markets tend to favor the known over the unknown." Evan is well informed about current events. Next to investments, politics is his avocation, and he often discusses its impact on the market. We've never had a meeting when he didn't steer the conversation to government affairs. I share an avid interest but worry that the distraction will leave little time to complete my review.

I glanced at my silver dollar-sized watch: our time is almost up. I had to keep Evan focused on my holdings so that I had a chance to share my phenomenal news.

"We're not seeing much in the way of great bargains at the moment, and while there may be some small changes that I recommend in the coming weeks, I don't see the need for any major alterations now."

Secure in his financial acumen; I said, "That's fine."

Closing my file, he looked up and said, "It looks like we've covered everything. Any questions?"

Time for my big announcement! "Cooper and I are getting married," I blurted.

Evan's eyebrows shot up. Cooper had accompanied me to several investment reviews. The men seemed to get along famously. Coop had been on his best behavior: personable, asked the right questions, kept quiet when necessary, and was respectful of Evan.

"Congratulations." His tone was less than sincere.

"Thanks, we're very happy."

"When's the wedding?"

"February seventh."

The wheels of my financial advisor's calculations turned in his head.

"Who is drawing up your prenuptial agreement?"

Crushed at having my happiness tempered by reason, I replied, "I don't need one."

"I've managed your money for the last seven years," he said, "What kind of advisor would I be if I didn't insist on a prenup? You have a lot to lose."

"Evan, this is the real thing. I have never been so in love. Cooper has given me no reason to doubt his integrity. In fact, he has confided the most personal details of his finances."

"I've seen a lot of money fall into the wrong hands," Evan warned.

His implication was unsettling. A disapproving frown creased the skin between Evan's eyes. He leaned forward. "Do you realize what is at stake? A divorce could cost you half of everything you own."

I drew back. "We would never divorce."

"I'm only looking out for your best interest."

"Evan, he's a sheriff. He wouldn't want anything that isn't his."

Evan folded his hands on his desk. "How long have you known him?"

"We've been living together almost a year."

"I urge you to do a prenup," Evan persisted, looking at me over the top of his glasses like my father used to when he was doling out advice. "If Cooper loves you as much as you say, he shouldn't have a problem."

I shook my head. He would be livid if I even mentioned the dreaded word. There was not a doubt in my mind that he'd walk. And I was not about to lose him.

Evan saw my resolve and knew his words were futile. I was offended that he doubted my judgment, and angry that he questioned Cooper's honor. No one, not even my trusted financial advisor, was going to stop my nuptials.

Part Two

Ten

Cooper and I were to exchange wedding vows at the Marshall County Courthouse on February seven. I envisioned a flawless ceremony; affirming our love surrounded by all our friends and family.

A fresh snow blanketed the winter landscape as Margo and I drove to the Sweet Shoppe to finalize plans. For this endeavor, we needed plenty of coffee and cinnamon rolls, dripping with icing. As we entered the familiar brick building on the corner, I could smell warm, made from scratch Danish and freshly brewed coffee. We sat in a booth near the foggy windows, leaving the counter stools available for the regular customers.

"Margo, I've never been this happy or this nervous," I fretted, biting into my sticky roll. "It takes most brides six months or longer to plan a wedding. I have six weeks."

Margo, my maid of honor and the driving force behind preparations, flipped open her notepad. "With your style and my organization, we've got it made."

"But your plate is full. You'll become Mrs. Sutherland the following week."

"You know me. I had my wedding planned before Michael popped the question."

We laughed.

She tapped her canary yellow notepad with its matching pen and checked off tasks completed.

"The date is set, arrangements made at the courthouse, friends and family invited." She looked up from her notes. "You've reserved Gorat's for the reception?"

"I booked the banquet room."

Steam rolled up from our mugs as the waitress refilled our coffee.

"When will your rings be ready?" Margo asked, tapping a sagging ash in the ash tray.

"We'll pick them up Saturday while we're in the city. Time's running out; I've got to find a dress."

"That will be today's priority," Margo said, jotting a reminder down with a businesslike flourish.

"I can't wait to see the red velvet dress you'll wear for your Valentine's Day wedding."

Margo smiled, "When I saw it. I just had to have it."

Lowering my voice, I said, "I must have a sexy nightgown."

"We'll buy the most seductive one we can find at Victoria's Secret." Margo's energy was contagious. As we paid our bill, she said, "Let's do what we do best – shop."

We headed to Cherées, Omaha's Saks Fifth Avenue, to find a classy wedding dress, any color but maroon. Two hours later, I had tried on every appropriate dress in the store. Nothing jumped out at me. I finally settled for a two-piece, winter-white knit suit and would accessorize with diamond and gold jewelry and cream pumps. My grandmother's wedding ring would be something old, my suit something new, and Margo's lacy garter borrowed and blue. A bouquet of white roses and lavender orchids would complete my ensemble.

At Victoria's Secret, Margo and I walked past the displays of beauty products, lotions, and perfumes, beyond the swimsuits and T-shirts, to the back of the store where they had the risqué sleep and loungewear concealed from the mall walkers and perverts. I had never seen that much pink. Margo held up a gorgeous silk and lace negligee, not pink, and smiled, "He'll die when he sees you in this."

I squinted, "Is that black or navy?"

"Navy and it's almost completely see-through."

We giggled our way to the check-out counter.

According to custom, Michael hosted a stag party for the groom in Woodland, and Margo stayed with me in the city. We threw on sweat pants and T-shirts, grabbed Dr. Peppers, and settled at the kitchen table for a gabfest.

"Everyone's been asking me for gift ideas," Margo said. "I suggested food."

"That's perfect," I laughed. "I hate to cook, and Cooper loves to eat."

We talked into the night. The conversation led to our first husbands. Margo lost Justin in a tragic car accident on his way home from work after five short, but joyful, years of marriage. I shared my last night with Boots…

"You're always gone. The kids never see you."

"Not again." He sighed and lit a cigarette. He leaned back in his red leather chair, feet on the ottoman.

I was on the paisley couch. Angry!

"Quiet down," he said. "Don't wake the kids!"

Lowering my voice, "Work is a necessity. The other activities that monopolize your time are not. It's football season. If there isn't a home game, you're glued to the T.V. all weekend. In spring and summer, it's horse races or golf. There is always something! I'm tired of you disappointing Mark."

He snapped up the newspaper. End of conversation.

I went to the kitchen, banged cupboard doors, and clanged dishes, mumbling under my breath. Stomping past my husband, I went to bed. Let him think about being more of a hands-on-dad. I fell asleep.

The hostile alarm clock awoke me from a deep sleep. I felt uneasy. I reached for Boots. His side of the bed was cold. He was a sound sleeper, rarely awakening without the alarm. The hall light was on. Something was wrong. In our sixteen-year marriage, I couldn't recall my frugal husband going to bed without turning the lights off and adjusting the thermostat. I called his name. No answer. I quickly grabbed my robe and hurried into the family room. I froze.

Boots was lying on the floor.

I screamed for our eleven-year-old son who was asleep in his bedroom off the family room. Mark ran in, his thick black hair sticking straight up. He saw his father.

Rushing to him, he knelt and put an ear to his chest.

"He's alive, Mom. He's alive," trying to convince us both.

Numb, barely able to dial, I called 911, then our family doctor. Our neighbors, Elaine and Sam, heard the sirens and dashed into the house. The paramedics confirmed what we knew but couldn't believe. I watched the men carefully place a sheet over my husband's lifeless body. I was deeply touched by the comment from one of them, "I'm sorry, Ma'am."

Hours of shock and confusion followed. I asked Elaine to call my best friend, Ruth, and Boots' sister Auddie, who would relay the heartbreaking news to their parents. Relieved at having something specific to do, Elaine took charge. Bad news travels quickly. Our rabbi and doctor arrived, followed by a steady stream of friends, a testament to their love and respect for Boots. Some were sobbing, others standing about unable to speak, still others attempting to comfort me – all expressing disbelief.

Several years earlier Boots was diagnosed with prostate cancer and underwent treatment. He had recently been declared cancer-free.

Our doctor said that an autopsy would be performed.

I approached the rabbi. "I was so wrong to call Mark. I'm afraid I've scarred him for life."

"You did the right thing," Rabbi Leibowitz comforted. "You needed your son."

Despite the chaos, Gail, thirteen, and Diane, four, were still asleep at the other end of the house. Worried that I had harmed Mark irreparably by my instinctive cry, I didn't want to botch telling the girls. I relayed the tragic news as gently as possible.

"It's not true! I don't believe you. Dad isn't dead," Gail screamed.

I put my arms around her. She pushed me away. She wanted her father.

I found Diane crouched behind the curtain under her little vanity clutching her favorite stuffed monkey, Charlie. She knew something bad had happened and that was her way of coping.

The autopsy revealed that Boots had died of heart failure. Only 43, he had the heart of a man twice his age.

"That makes me so sad," Margo said. "It reminds me of Justin. We were only married five years when I got the call about the accident."

"We've weathered many storms. It's our turn to be happy."

Our wedding day dawned unseasonably warm for February in Nebraska. It was a perfect day to begin married life. I stretched, smiled, and pushed back the covers, then took a long steamy shower, thinking about the day and night ahead. I never doubted my decision to tie the knot. I felt so alive in Cooper's presence and drawn to his masculinity and charisma that I overlooked his narcissistic traits, his inflated ego, and his constant need to be the center of attention, dominating every conversation.

After dressing in jeans and a long-sleeved sweatshirt, I hurried downstairs. Margo had started the coffee, and we enjoyed a relaxing breakfast of orange juice, coffee, bagels, and small talk. The calm wouldn't last long.

While the sun rose through billowy clouds, I carefully applied makeup and hung my suit in Margo's car. Finally, we were on our way. As Margo drove, she lit a cigarette and nervously rattled a mental checklist. "I hope the flowers arrive on time. The license! Where's the marriage license?"

"Calm down. I've got it right here in my purse."

"Are you sure Cooper will remember the rings?"

"I'm not going to worry about it. Rings or no rings we're getting married today. If he forgets, we'll borrow someone else's. Probably yours."

At the courthouse, I hurried in the opposite direction, away from her nervousness. I changed into my suit, thankful I didn't jab a fingernail through my hose and run them and touched up my lipstick in the ladies' room. Diane poked her head in the door, "I see you didn't back out." She smoothed my blush and fluffed my hair. Hugging me, she said in a conspiratorial whisper, "Last chance to make a getaway. I'll drive." Then she saw the sparkle in my eyes. "Mom, you look beautiful."

Blinded by love, I felt calm as I looked for Cooper. I found my groom, pacing like a race horse, at the courtroom door. He looked handsome in his black suit. The white rose boutonniere on his lapel resembled a smattering of cake frosting. Oh, how I loved that man.

"Be careful, you'll wear a hole in the floor," I said smiling.

He smiled back. Putting his arm around me, he said, "You look great."

Our guests began arriving. It was a small intimate ceremony with a few close friends. We greeted everyone as they entered. Jake slapped Coop on the back, "Bear, your new uniform becomes you." Cooper's best man Michael, the image of actor Lee Marvin, looked sharp in his crisp navy suit. My maid of honor Margo, wearing a tailored light blue dress, mingled with the guests.

At 10:55 a.m. Cooper opened the courtroom door and bellowed, "Come on, woman. Let's get hitched." We all laughed at his red neck language.

Cooper and I, flanked by Margo and Michael, faced the bench. The judge entered from his chambers and took his position in front of us. He spoke of love and commitment. I hung on every word. Cooper remembered the rings; we slid sparkling diamond bands, custom designed at Borsheim's, on each other's fingers.

With all my heart I said, "I do." Cooper echoed. My spirits soared.

"I now pronounce you husband and wife."

We kissed passionately. I tossed my bouquet to Margo.

We had hired Sebastian Photography to provide a professional keepsake of our momentous day. Subby resembled actor Danny DeVito and stood about a foot shorter than my husband. Subby tried comedy to get smiles on everyone's faces. He stepped back, then stepped back a little more and quipped "Suck it in big boy, or this will have to be a panoramic shot."

My happy groom became so angry I was afraid he'd grab the gun in his boot. "Listen, you sawed off little runt, shut your mouth before I shut it for you!" His voice boomed so loud it echoed through the corridors of the courthouse.

Michael and Jake's mouths were in a perfect 'O'; eyes wide. They knew what that threat meant. Their wives avoided eye contact with me and stared at the floor as if they were embarrassed. I wanted to crawl under a bench.

Subby, attempting to make the best of a bad situation, adjusted his lens and snapped about a dozen pictures. I'm sure he didn't want to find himself in a headlock with my husband and then handcuffed in the backseat of our car. I smiled. The moment was supposed to be storybook perfect. We made it through the photo session with no assaults or injuries – other than Subby's pride.

Why didn't we elope?

Cooper and I made the thirty-minute drive to Omaha in strained silence. I could tell he was holding on to his anger by the way he clenched his jaw and gripped the steering wheel. We stopped at my house to freshen up before heading to the reception, where all our guests had already gathered at the bar discussing the "beautiful" photo-op. Fortunately, Cooper had calmed down before we joined them.

As I requested, Gorat's staff had decorated the banquet room. The tables, covered with white linen cloths, were positioned in a u-shape. Cooper and I sat at the head. Small bouquets of yellow and white carnations and baby's breath, laced with white satin ribbon, adorned each table. Everyone enjoyed themselves with lively conversation. Our guests toasted us, giving congratulatory hugs and best wishes. Juicy filets that melted in our mouths and double chocolate cake ended the day on a sweeter note.

Our honeymoon suite was the bedroom at my house. I slipped into my seductive negligee and sprayed White Shoulders behind my ears and between my breasts and made my grand entrance.

Cooper lounged naked on the bed. "I've got a sore throat," he complained.

The needle scratched across the record of violins playing in my head. I threw on my terry cloth robe. "I'll get the Chloraseptic spray and aspirin. We'll celebrate tomorrow."

"I can't believe you're turning me down," he snapped. "I said my throat is sore. I didn't say my dick is broken. Get over here!"

My robe hit the floor. This was my husband – the love of my life.

When we returned to the farm early Sunday, I was looking forward to the barbecue Margo and Michael were hosting in our honor. Six couples were invited to help us celebrate.

I dressed in a new pair of jeans and a cream-colored blouse with lace inlay and red pumps and belt. I put on lipstick at the bathroom mirror and stepped into the bedroom to check Coop's progress. He was wearing his trademark flannel shirt and faded jeans.

"You're the guest of honor. You can't dress like that."

His blue eyes bore into mine, "The hell I can't! No woman tells me what to wear!"

I took a step back. His rage shocked me. It was completely disproportionate to my comment. He acted as though I had said, "You country hick. You look like you're going to the south 40 to feed cattle."

"I'm sorry, honey. I didn't mean to upset you." Me and my big mouth.

The ride to Margo and Michael's home was unbearably tense. Afraid that Cooper would be on the warpath the entire evening, I fought back the tears. I wanted my husband to take my hand as I stepped out of the car into a pile of snow, but he marched ahead. My foot slammed into the porch step. I grabbed the railing and followed.

It was a Martha Stewart 'gone country' party. Above the front door, a red and white checkered banner proclaimed, "Congratulations Mr. and Mrs. Bear." A hay bale with green foliage decorated the entrance.

Margo and Michael greeted us warmly. Faith Hill's song, *Piece of My Heart,* played in the background as if playing out the day's events. *"Break another little piece of my heart now, baby 'cause you know you got it if it makes you feel good."*

"Excuse me. My baked beans are going to burn," Margo said, blowing me an air kiss.

Michael pumped Cooper's hand. "Bear, you did it. You finally made an honest woman out of her. Here's to the end of your bachelor days." He handed Cooper a beer and raised his glass.

"Your ball and chain go on Thursday," Cooper joked, clinking his beer with Michael's.

I had pictured us making the rounds as Sheriff and Mrs. Cowan, basking in the spotlight. Our friends greeted me, but it was obvious there was something wrong; Cooper kept his distance and did not speak to me the entire evening. He didn't even look at me. Humiliated, I made my way to the couch. I sat heartbroken and alone, in the corner near the fireplace, afraid to talk for fear the tears would flow. Coop's behavior was not normal. Why was he punishing me for wanting him to look nice?

Jake gave Coop a congratulatory handshake. "I'll never understand why a good-looking woman like Ann puts up with you," Cooper teased.

He sat down across the room from me, saying, "How about bringing your chainsaw to the farm to help me cut down some trees? I'm getting low on firewood. I'll stop by, and we'll finish your fence."

Coop had a bevy of cronies, not only locally, but throughout the country. Besides their bragging barter and tall tales of female conquests, they were always available to chop wood or play backyard mechanic on someone's vehicle. There was an unspoken ironclad rule: Coop was the leader.

I couldn't join in the spirited banter. Cooper had shut me out. Did his attitude imply that he wanted nothing more to do with me and would again send me packing on our wedding weekend?

Margo outdid herself with the decorations and food: slow-cooked barbecue brisket, her signature baked beans, and potato salad. Everyone had a great time – except me.

After the last guest had departed, Cooper shrugged into his black leather jacket and said, "Let's go." He went to the car without me. Holding the railing tight, I descended into blackness. I never had night vision. Fortunately, I knew that there were five steps to their sidewalk, and felt each one with my toes. I walked toward the headlights, hoping I wouldn't trip over anything and end up face down in a snowbank. There was total silence on the ride home. As we prepared for bed, the silent treatment persisted. He turned his back and fell asleep.

Cooper appeared at breakfast pressed, polished, and ready for crime-stopping, wearing his wedding band. After Corn Flakes and coffee, he kissed me ardently and left. The smell of Old Spice lingered in the air. The truck tires crunched gravel out to the road as he drove off to his day.

The kiss. Rays of sun splashed onto the tablecloth. I collapsed into a chair. A bird, perched on a tree limb scolded. A dark flock of shadows flapped across the table. Small birds chirped at the feeder.

It was the first day of the rest of my marriage. I hummed while washing the dishes. There is a reason the ceremony includes for better or worse. It's going to be a wonderful night.

Eleven

A twenty-five mile per hour wind blew leaves from the trees as Cooper and I hastily left the farm. An afternoon thunderstorm was moving in. Big dark twists of clouds mounted over the countryside, threatening severe weather: the kind of atmosphere that forms tornadoes on the plains. Fat drops of rain splashed across the windshield.

The acute pain in Cooper's back, his bulk, and labored breathing made it difficult for him to settle behind the steering wheel. He gripped it tightly, knuckles turning white as he sped like a demolition derby driver toward Midlands Hospital. He had thrown his back out cleaning the horse stables in the barn, and the shooting pain had his undivided attention. The car fishtailed with each muscle spasm.

"They say no land is worth dying for because it's the only thing that lasts," he whimpered.

I looked at him. "What?" unsure if I'd heard correctly. What was he trying to say?

"I've had a will drawn up," he moaned as if he had an hour left to live. "If anything happens to me, you inherit the farm. I hope you'll live here and look after it like I do." I stared at Cooper's profile. His jaw muscle twitched. My eyes filled with tears. I couldn't imagine a future without him; of anything tragic ever happening. Obviously, he was thinking ahead to make sure that his farm didn't fall into the wrong hands; that it would continue to prosper. I pictured myself as Coop's devoted and unselfish widow – giving up life in the city to honor his memory and continue his legacy raising crops.

"Nothing means more to me than my land and you," Cooper said, his eyes tearing. I wasn't sure if the tears were from sentiment or pain. I felt like the most important person in his world. He trusted me with his most precious possession. He had already made it clear that it would take his passing for him to consider parting with his blue ribbon real estate. Did he think that a backache would really put him in his grave?

While Cooper was married to his first wife Karen, they and their infant son returned from Wyoming to live in Woodland. They'd purchased 160 acres outside of town at an auction. The house, advertised as a fixer-upper, was so dilapidated that he bought the property for a song. It needed paint, Lysol, Clorox, and lots of TLC. They worked tirelessly to renovate the run-down house, replacing sagging floorboards, cracked windows, torn screens, and the roof. They sanded the woodwork and refinished the floors with a glossy dark walnut stain. He had toiled over and treasured the property, removing overgrown trees and bushes, and planting a lush green lawn where nothing but weeds had taken over. His unexpected generosity in his last will and testament proved that when the chips were down, I had his everlasting love.

I never saw the will but didn't doubt that it existed.

When I was hurting, "in sickness" meant nothing to Cooper. At the onset of menopause, I was near tears, doubled over with pain in my lower abdomen. Cooper was working in the yard. I opened the back door and called to him. "I feel like I'm hemorrhaging. Can you *please* take me to my doctor?"

He stopped digging, wiped his brow with the back of his hand, leaving a dirt smear across his forehead. He glared at me, "Suck it up. You act like this is your first period. Hell, I'm out here working my ass off with a broken back, and I have to report for shift at 3:00. You don't hear me bitching." I dragged myself back to the heating pad and bed wishing for anything to kill the burning pain in my middle.

Two days later, with cramping so bad it was like labor pains, he begrudgingly drove me to the doctor who recommended a D&C. After surgery, my dismissal orders stated rest and abstinence for seven days. Doctor Harlow cautioned, "Follow my instructions, or you will be back with the possibility of a complete or partial hysterectomy." By mid-week, Cooper couldn't wait and forced himself on me – as if he owned me. I pleaded with him to stop, but his testosterone level and need to control had peaked. I had no free will as he straddled me, and I was afraid to deny him. I felt helpless; powerless against him. Trapped beneath his 240-pound body, I balled the sheets in my fists and cried as my husband raped me.

Cooper had crossed a line. The verbal abuse was now growing into a physical phase. I had never been taught to defend myself. I should have been, but not from strangers who might attack me – from those who were closest to me who appeared to have my best interest at heart.

The emergency aide, red-faced from wrestling Cooper's bulk into a wheelchair, had assisted Diane. Cooper didn't notice the cynical look that widened my eyes. After berating Diane, he was experiencing the same trauma and would not respond kindly to being called a big baby. It was not the time to bring it up, but the thought made me smirk. Obviously, he was hurting and would lash out at anyone who questioned his cries for help.

Cooper could not see himself playing out the same medical drama for which he had castigated Diane. If there was ever an instance where the concept of Karma was in play, this was it. Cooper wasn't cognizant of the situation's irony.

Following a battery of x-rays and tests, physicians discovered two ruptured discs in Coopers' already broken back. When the doctor released Cooper with a shoebox full of prescriptions and orders to rest, he expected me to fawn over and nurse him back to health. It was my job to tolerate his crabbiness while making sure he took his medication on time, fetch his water, serve his meals in his rocker, massage his back, and perform my wifely duties – not an easy task when your partner is incapacitated. That never stopped him. As much as I needed and enjoyed intimacy, I never wanted to feel like it was an obligation. Would it hurt to wait till he healed? He grumbled about needing a bed with adequate support. "Babe, you know how much better I'd feel." I called local medical supply stores and had an adjustable bed delivered to my house; his house was too small to accommodate a bed with levers and gears to support preferred positions. I would prove my profound love for him, thus erasing his shitty childhood.

Twelve

Cooper and I sat in Margo and Michael's kitchen where the coffee pot was always on. Painted country blue, the room was decorated with ruffled cream curtains and navy accents. The motif spilled over to the salt and pepper shakers, light switches, napkin and paper towel holders. From the basement, I heard Bon Jovi belting his latest hit. Michael's teenage daughter was jamming on her stereo.

"Holly," he called, "turn the music down."

"Commissioner Sutherland," Cooper said, once the singing had softened. "Now that's got a nice ring to it!"

We looked at Cooper, surprised.

His chair creaked as he leaned back, "Ed Novacek isn't going to run for re-election."

"Really?" I asked, warming my hands on my coffee mug.

"He and Blanche bought a condo in Florida. They're going to be snowbirds. I'll miss the old man. Margo, the job is there for the taking. Your butt is just right for that seat."

The prospect didn't appeal to her. She shook her head, lighting a cigarette from the end of her last with trembling hands. "I've never considered running for public office."

"Why not?" Cooper said, "You are smart as a whip. A natural."

"I've been thinking about returning to college to earn my degree. I had two years left when I quit to marry Michael."

"What's stopping you?" I asked, wondering why she hadn't mentioned pursuing this goal. We had always shared everything.

"The remote commute; long stretches of deserted highway, especially in bad weather."

Coop looked at her sideways through squinty eyes. She had not convinced him that she couldn't be swayed.

"Hell, Margo, you can exercise your mental muscle running the county. Everything from businesses to roads, to taxes, is under the commissioners' jurisdiction. We'll clean up this place."

Michael, our lanky waiter, refilled our cups. Taking a chair across from Cooper, he asked, "Hey, Bear, how much time away from the house are we talking? I don't want my wife gone all the time. Holly can't be trusted alone for long."

"Margo can work from this kitchen table," he palmed it for emphasis, "attend some meetings and make a few public appearances here and there. Best of all, she'll have the services of my humble department. Piece of cake."

Margo pushed her chair back; walked to the counter, and began pacing the room. "What if no one votes for me?" she fretted.

Cooper exhaled. "I'll take care of that," he said confidently. "I didn't steer you wrong with Michael, and I'm not about to now."

"Margo, you're such a smart money manager," I chimed in, the dutiful wife, supporting my husband, and encouraging my best friend.

Michael joined the volley. "She saved my credit and will do the same for Marshall County."

I recalled her taking charge of Michael's finances shortly after she moved in with him. She wasn't about to marry a man who had so many outstanding debts. "Make a list of all your bills," she'd instructed. He did, starting with one of his motorcycles. He wasn't allowed to buy anything else until the bills were paid in full. She gave him enough cash each day to buy lunch. Michael chafed at the restriction, but like me, it was easier to give in and avoid friction.

Margo emptied the overflowing ashtrays, wiped them clean with a rag, and looked around the kitchen; spotless, sparkling counter tops, everything in its place; not a crumb on the floor – so clean you could eat off it. "This house is a big responsibility. I can't count on Michael and Holly to pick up after themselves, and I refuse to let it go."

"There will be plenty of time for your compulsive cleaning," Cooper said, grinning to soften the needle.

It's a win-win," I coaxed. "You get paid to stay home with Holly and help run the county."

Later I learned that it's advantageous for a sheriff to have a "friend" on the county board. Everything my husband schemed was with his ends in mind. I wasn't the only impressionable one. He was a pro at spotting compliant individuals who would do his bidding. In my innocence, I did not sense Cooper's underlying deception, or I would not have gone along with his pitch.

Margo took Cooper's bait like a mouse to cheese and sped to the courthouse to make her candidacy official. I never understood how one goes from obtaining a Bachelor of Fine Arts degree to running for public office in a twenty-minute conversation. Did she thoroughly think about this? Her campaign consisted of befriending neighbors, postmen, business owners, the guy behind the counter at the dry cleaners, and school teachers to gain their votes.

The sheriff called in a few favors. Harriet Whitfield, the Ford dealer's wife, was a kleptomaniac. While she stuffed a shopping bag and her purse with perfumes, cosmetics, and sweaters, the local merchants looked the other way. Store owners tallied the price of the items and sent bills to Miles, who immediately made good on her take. William Walsh, a highly-respected attorney, had just built a million-dollar home at the lake. Cooper gave his seventeen-year-old daughter a get-out-of-jail-free card instead of arresting her for MIP (Minor in possession), saving their family public humiliation.

The election was a shoo-in. Ordinarily overly skittish, Margo went from homemaker to lawmaker with gusto. We toasted her victory with coffee in their cozy kitchen.

It took only a few weeks for her euphoria to dissipate. She had landed under Cooper's boot – answering to him for the duration of her term and beyond.

Her responsibilities included attending public forums. One day she was to be the guest speaker at Woodland's Chamber of Commerce monthly meeting. Practicing in front of her hall mirror, she removed cat hair from her coral linen suit with a lint roller. Cooper had settled on the overstuffed chair in the living room; his long legs stretched out in front of him. Sipping coffee, he coached.

She sat down on the couch and rummaged through her purse – crumpling old grocery store receipts and tissues. "There's going to be a lot of opposition to Wal-Mart's proposal to build in Woodland," Margo brooded.

"Don't back down," Cooper instructed, giving her his cop-glare. "Too much money is spent outside of our community."

"The local business owners will hate me."

"You didn't run for office to make friends. It will create jobs and bring revenue into the county, something that is sorely needed. Les Katz, the big shot at Pac A Sac, and Lucy Fontane, the bitch at Lucy's Boutique, will have to lower prices or close their doors."

Every morning Cooper clocked in at the sheriff's department. Unless there was a problem needing his attention, unlikely in this sleepy county, he headed to Margo's house where they huddled over business like crime conspirators.

Before meeting our husbands, it was common for Margo and me to gab three or four times a day. Soon after we moved to Woodland, a distance had begun to grow. She seldom called me anymore. The friendship that we shared had shifted. She spent more of her free time with her neighbor Frances; exchanging recipes and cleaning chickens – of all things! I missed Margo.

On my calls to her, I could tell by the edge in her voice if my man in uniform was there. Stranded at the farm, I imagined the worst-case scenario. Were they just exchanging the latest gossip or had they transferred county business to the bedroom? He hadn't gone to Commissioner Novacek's house every day. Distrust between Margo and me had taken root. I knew that Cooper was reveling in the torturous thoughts running through my head, picturing them in a darkened room under the sheets. What did he have to gain from playing this game? If he had so much time on his hands, why wasn't he home with me?

Margo and I had always turned to one another in times of trouble. Now she was part of my desperation. I could still call her and share my concerns about Cooper's erratic behavior, and she revealed her worries about county business. "You should see my desk. The paperwork is piling up about the potholes in town." But the bond between us had begun to fray when we moved to Woodland.

Margo now walked a fine line between complying with Cooper's demands and maintaining our friendship. At lunch one day in her kitchen, she suddenly put her half-eaten sandwich on the plate. Her eyes looked like those of a wild animal that had gotten its leg caught in a steel trap. "You don't know how afraid I am of Cooper."

I almost choked on my Dr. Pepper. "What are you saying? Why?"

"As an officer of the law, he has access to confidential information. That's how he controls everyone. If I don't follow his orders, he'll say I misused the authority of the position. I'll get sued."

Margo had a paralyzing fear of losing her nest egg through court action. She had inherited a respectable sum of money when her husband died and would take whatever measures necessary to protect it.

Cooper looked for inconsistencies in the stories of others. He worked tirelessly to expose the skeletons in their closets. He was Marshall County's J. Edgar Hoover. He knew who slept with whom and who wanted to sleep with whom (including himself). He was a walking courthouse records room and could repeat every burglary, homicide, and shoplifting case that had occurred in the town in the past twenty years. He also played cards and drank coffee with every sheriff, deputy, and judge in each case.

"He wouldn't do that. You and Michael are our best friends. The job isn't worth it," I said.

Her hand shook as she lit another cigarette. "I don't care about the stupid job. I wish I had never been elected."

The realization that she was now working for the sheriff while appearing to have the best interests of the county at heart overshadowed any prestige and excitement that Cooper had promised. Her actions and decisions affected lives and not always in a positive way. My husband was a master manipulator.

Cooper was my ride home. He pulled up promptly at 3:15.

Margo took my arm as I headed for the side door. "Be careful of the open stairs. Stay close to the wall."

On the way to the farm, I gazed at his profile, with automobiles and telephone poles whipping past like images on a silent movie screen. He gets his way too easily. The reality that neither my marriage nor my friendship was as solid as I had once believed made me feel completely alone.

Thirteen

One morning while Cooper was dousing his Cheerios with sugar, he surprised me with an out-of-the-blue compliment, "Babe, it's a waste of a brilliant mind that you don't work."

I nearly sprayed my drink of coffee everywhere! What did he just say? Anytime Cooper told me how smart I was, my checkbook had to take cover. He was just as inclined to speak to me in a condescending manner, *'Hundred dollar words don't work on me.'*

I smiled. "Flattery will get you everywhere." As we continued our morning routine, Cooper did not say anything more about my mind or my working. We sipped coffee while he searched the obituaries in the Woodland Herald for clues to property that might come to market. There was local farmland Cooper coveted. Places where the young people had gone away to make their lives in the city, and he could approach the inheritors while they were in the clutches of grief and might be persuaded to sell out cheap.

He looked up, "I don't know what I'd do if I didn't have the crime stopper crew to run."

"With your brains and ability, you could be the sheriff of Douglas County." How could I have been so naïve to think he could get criminal activity under control in the largest county in Nebraska? Marshall County, more like Mayberry, was his beat. But Crips and Bloods was a deadly issue.

"Flattery will get you everywhere," he said with the grin that always made me feel special. He lit a cigarette and leaned back with an air of self-satisfaction. "I'd rather be a big frog in a little pond. The fewer people I oversee, the tighter rein I can keep." There was no slack in the leash he had on Commissioner Sutherland – and me.

"You never miss a day of work," I said.

"Only when my back goes out."

"I envy you. It must be rewarding to have a job that you love."

"It wasn't handed to me. I've paid my dues."

Before we met, Cooper had been a decorated police officer at the end of his twelfth year and wanted to move up. He had gone through extensive physical conditioning to develop strength and stamina, necessary for promotion. Then he filed the required paperwork and began campaigning. His talkative nature coupled with his size were qualities in his favor for a lawman. He easily intimidated and beat out the competition.

Dawn was creeping across the horizon, and the birds were beginning to sing as Cooper prepared to meet the day. He mashed out his cigarette, strapped on his heavy gun belt, and topped off his coffee. Kissing me, he said, "Talk to you later."

As long as I felt no tension between us, beyond the fear of censure I endured daily, I was content at the farm. However, I had a lot of time on my hands.

Having finished my tasks: cleaning the kitchen, emptying the overflowing smelly ashtrays, feeding the dogs, I went to the parlor and watched the Today show. I read until my eyes rebelled at the brink of a migraine and then rode my stationary bike. Weather permitting, I'd walk the gravel road bordering the farm with my faithful companions at my side. I made detailed notes for stuff to attend to on my weekly trip to the city. Cooper's "waste of a brilliant mind" observation motivated me to consider my options. The desire for self-improvement stirred while I folded laundry, a mindless chore. I didn't want just to be a wife. I wanted to do something with my life.

Growing up, I'd never considered a specific job or profession. When I was in high school, if algebra or geometry were difficult or a science project boring, which it usually was, my parents never gave me the 'We're not quitters' speech. They either let me quit, or Dad did the assignment for me. Not a good example.

At fourteen, I worked for my father part-time, answering the phone and filling in behind the counter at his lumber company. Dad was also a proponent of lessons from an unbiased boss. The summer of my sweet sixteenth, he steered me to a job at a women's clothing store. I loved choosing new apparel for customers – learning everyone's preference and seeing their pleasure when I found them the perfect outfit. Competing with other clerks was a challenge I met head-on. I was proud when, after only a few weeks, I was the number one commission earner.

At eighteen I was off to college full-time and took summer classes as well, so like most of the female student body, I didn't work. I was single-minded about one thing, and it wasn't a career. Men and whom I would marry was as far as I looked into my future. I graduated from college with a degree in Communications the semester following my marriage to Boots. I chose this field because I'd been in speech and drama during elementary and high school, and according to Mom, Dad always said that I expressed myself well.

As a young mother, I had many hours to brood over den mother responsibilities, car pools, and science experiments exploding in my kitchen. My children's minor problems could easily escalate into larger issues for me than if I had been working. Unfortunately, I had no burning passion. Boots and I didn't need the money. He and his father were partners in a successful insurance agency.

After sixteen years of marriage Boots died of a heart attack. His love extended beyond the grave. There aren't many women in their mid-thirties whose husbands die and leave them financially secure. It was a mixed blessing. Work would have given me a reprieve from worrying about the children and a focus other than finding another husband. Proving to myself that I could hold a job would have boosted my self-confidence and provided a different set of survival skills. In my naiveté, I thought I would achieve complete happiness only through romance. Some of my life choices might have been different.

I have always admired my sister, Joany and my son, Mark, who knew early in life the careers they wanted to pursue and were willing to do the hard work to achieve them. Joany was a feminist pioneer in the cinema profession.

When Mark was eleven, I introduced him to the stock market. He studied books on investments and was immediately fascinated with strategies, bonds, capital gains, and liquidations. He still immerses himself in economics, and I'm proud to say works hard and is very knowledgeable about stocks.

I reflected on my first attempt to earn an advanced degree during my marriage to Donald. Friends said, "You've missed your calling. With your insight and ability to express yourself, you should be a therapist – or a politician."

Fortunately, I passed the entrance exam and was admitted to the Master's Program in Counseling and Guidance at the same university where Donald taught. I also joined an outside therapy class to learn the practical side of counseling. We role-played, taking turns as therapist and patient. After listening to people's problems all day, I knew I had chosen the wrong profession. It was boring and reminded me of my life. I accumulated six credit hours and exited the program. Soon after, I took an interesting part-time job working in the Resource Center at the college nearby, addressing women's issues. I met women who were coming out of their husbands' shadow and following their goals. I made new and stimulating friendships.

Months after Boots died, I had started writing a rough draft for a book about widowhood to challenge misconceptions held by society: "It's easier to be a divorcee than a widow," or "It never gets any better." Sixty widows of all ages had shared their experiences in taped interviews. I had completed nine chapters. When Donald asked for a divorce, I closed the pages of my manuscript, placed them in the back of the file cabinet, and walked away. Out of spite, I ignored his encouraging words, "Finish your book. It's good." I only hurt myself.

I still had a longing for higher education and decided to seek a Masters in History with an English minor. History, particularly American, had always fascinated me, and because I already attempted to complete a book, English seemed a logical choice.

 Now I was excited at the prospect of obtaining a Master's Degree. I looked forward to studying the great works of literature written by Hemingway, Steinbeck, and Nebraska's own, Willa Cather.

I began to formulate a plan, wisely cautious. Even though Cooper had encouraged me to look further than the gravel lane, it was a given that anything that interfered with my absolute and total attention and services would be prohibited. Any inconvenience to Cooper would bring my budding aspirations to a screeching halt. I had to anticipate his objections and provide solutions to sell him on my intentions.

The first obstacle was the eighteen miles to campus. *'The half hour commute – long stretches of deserted highway, especially in bad weather.'* How would I get there? Recently I had hired Janet to take me to the city once a week, between Cooper's and my weekend excursions. I would talk to her about the possibility of additional chauffeuring. Would a degree be worth the visual pressure? I hoped to be able to manage the required reading with my magnifiers.

I shook off the negative thoughts. Summer had eased into fall, my favorite time of year when everything seemed possible. The vivid colored autumn leaves cartwheeled across the road. Walking was especially pleasurable on cool, crisp mornings. Niki, Duchess, and I felt energized. I put my plan into action and called Nebraska University to find out their requirements.

I prepared for Cooper to come home, making sure everything was perfect. The fire in the wood stove crackled, just the way he liked it, and a chicken baking in the oven filled the kitchen with a delicious aroma. Finally, I heard the distinctive rumble of his pickup on the gravel drive. Niki and Duchess ran to the door. Cooper patted them on their heads, greeted me with a kiss, and then went to change. His cheerful mood was encouraging. I poured his coffee while he threw on Levi's and a flannel shirt. He lit a cigarette, took a sip, and began a recap of his day. It consisted of a little truth, lots of gossip, and imagination sprinkled with insights so profound that I remember them to this day.

I waited for the right moment. "You told me that my mind is going to waste," I said, with as much courage as I could muster.

"That's right." He raised an eyebrow.

I took a deep breath. "I'm thinking about going to the university to earn my masters."

Cooper glared at me, "How the hell are you going to get there?"

Here we go. "I talked to Janet." My courage was waning.

"What about me?" His voice was rising. "How am I supposed to get along?"

"I'll take one class and be gone only two mornings a week. You'll be at work."

"So instead of watching a movie with me at night, your face will be buried in a damn book?"

He jumped up, shoving his chair so hard it hit the wall. I flinched. The dogs cowered to the bedroom, tails between their legs. The coffee spilled, making a puddle on the table, and dripping onto the floor. Cooper's face was as red as his hair. The vein in the middle of his forehead bulged.

"Typical selfish woman! Haven't you got enough to do here? I should have known you'd pull this shit."

He stormed out the door. I heard what sounded like the rake crashing against the tractor and him kicking the wheelbarrow. I hoped nothing would fly through the window in my direction.

I was angry that Cooper talked out of both sides of his mouth. I had expected some resistance, but not a meltdown. Even though employment in the outside world had been his idea, it made no difference how carefully I had planned. Cooper didn't care that I might have a dream. He was proud of my mind if it didn't inconvenience nor threaten him.

For the first time, his tantrum didn't bring me to tears. I didn't beg forgiveness or break into a sweat and feel sick, nor did I run to the phone and call my friends. I looked at my husband objectively and recognized his instability. I no longer gazed with blind adoration, but I still loved him.

I cleaned up the coffee and went about the routine of preparing dinner. Coop returned twenty minutes later. "I'm sorry." He went back outside to clean up his mess. That was the only time in our years together that he apologized.

What did his 'I'm sorry' really mean? Sorry he lost his temper? Sorry for the mess he made of the dining room? Sorry that he ever told me my mind was going to waste? Was Cooper afraid that if I ventured outside the farm that he'd lose control of me?

My new-found confidence had nothing to do with his uncharacteristic remorse. His selfish reaction was predictable but so bizarre that I felt a strength I hadn't realized I possessed. Cooper's objections were not the main reason I waffled and canceled my plan. I didn't have the drive to pursue this goal. It is one thing to talk tough and another to step into the ring.

Fourteen

While riding my stationary bike, high on endorphins, I daydreamed about our mind-blowing sex last night and Cooper's passionate words, "You're the only woman I've ever loved. I can't live without you." We had lain close together in the dark; spent and satisfied.

So, of course, when we woke up the next morning, we were all smiles and butterfly kisses. I had a glow about me, and I'm sure all the guys at work kidded Cooper about getting lucky last night. This thought put a smile on my face. When he kissed me goodbye, I pressed up against him; it was an unspoken promise of a repeat tonight.

The ring of the telephone cut short my daydreaming and peddling. I hated interrupting my workout. But I better answer – it's probably Cooper. I stepped carefully around the rocker to avoid tripping and answered on the fifth ring.

"What the hell took you so long?" Cooper barked.

"I was riding my bike," I said breathlessly. "Can I call you back in twenty minutes?"

"Your exercise is more important than me?"

The anger in his voice was a harsh contrast to the heartfelt midnight nothings he'd whispered in my ear the night before.

"Of course not, I always look forward to your calls. They're the highlight of my day," I said, hoping I sounded genuine, so as not to anger him more.

"You could have fooled me!" The phone slammed in my ear. I sat alone in the kitchen fuming over his selfishness. Why couldn't I finish my exercises without him exploding? For our marriage to survive, I sacrificed myself. When Coop was mad at me, I didn't wait for his punishment; I inflicted it. I walked away from my workout and turned my back on my aspiration to obtain a master's degree: self-sabotage. Instead of climbing back on the bike, as I should have, I remained on the stool, breathing slowly, to calm my shakiness.

Feeling defeated by his reaction and anxious that his foul mood would continue all day, I turned on the television in the parlor and heard applause at the beginning of a popular talk show. Sitting down in Cooper's rocker, I realized I'd forgotten my Dr. Pepper on the kitchen counter. As I rose to retrieve it, the words coming from the TV stopped me.

"Addictive love works like any other addiction, whether it is to alcohol, drugs, gambling, or food. There is a compulsive, driven need for the other person. A woman in an addictive love relationship, experiences intense pain and suffering when she is deprived of her partner; she feels that she cannot live without him. The relationship provides a high that nothing else matches. In order to get those highs, she will tolerate a great deal of abusive treatment. This sort of addiction makes the woman fiercely dependent on her partner."

I put my hand on my forehead and stared at the woman in disbelief. She was describing me. I was an addict and Cooper was my drug.

An unpretentious brunette with a sweet smile and compassionate, expressive voice was promoting her book, *Men Who Hate Women and the Women Who Love Them*. Dr. Susan Forward, a therapist, knew from her practice, calls to her radio show, and personal experience that domestic violence had soared to epidemic proportions.

She discussed her theory of Dr. Jekyll/Mr. Hyde behavior. Initially Dr. Jekyll searches for a compliant woman who dreams of being swept off her feet by Prince Charming. He wines and dines her, making her feel cherished in a way that she always envisioned love should be.

While her eyes are glazed over, she gets her first jolt of Mr. Hyde's dark personality. In his obsession to control, he tests her submissiveness. He might recommend growing her hair longer for a more youthful look or suggest a different way to dress. '*That maroon blouse doesn't look good on you! It makes you look old.*' His methodology is to weaken and program her to his specifications – all with his own needs in mind. If she acquiesces, he quickly moves on to dating exclusively, living together or perhaps convinces her to join him in a business venture. He monopolizes her time. If she refuses his recommendations or attempts to break up, he charms, cajoles, and is not above crocodile tears. As a last resort, he stalks. She is very fortunate if Mr. Hyde decides that she isn't worth more of his time and he moves on to someone more malleable.

According to Dr. Forward, my husband fit the profile of a misogynist, a man who needs to control to compensate for his insecurities. She explained in layman's terms that something was wrong with him and gave the symptoms a name. Her theory eased my feelings of responsibility for triggering his outbursts. I was relieved that there was a psychological explanation for his behavior and mine. She stressed that before any of us can change a relationship, we must understand what is occurring in it. But understanding is not enough. For our lives to improve, we must be open to changing ourselves.

Dr. Forward's words reached me with an impact that cautions from friends, family, or my financial advisor never had. Maybe it was because the author was a psychologist in my living room, with the weight of wisdom in her words. The epiphany was powerful. Seeing the dynamics of a dysfunctional relationship expressed so clearly gave me hope that I could turn my marriage around. I left my Dr. Pepper sweating on the counter as I rifled through the desk drawer for my Big Chief tablet and a pen to write down the information.

I couldn't wait to get my hands on Dr. Forward's book. I hoped it would provide the tools to change Cooper's volatile behavior and my submissiveness. I had to be careful. If it landed in his hands, the title alone would make his blood boil. I was willing to take the risk because nothing was more important to me than his love.

The light at the end of the tunnel, though weak, was on.

Fifteen

On our next trip to the city, I had two tasks: purchasing *Men Who Hate Women* and confronting Cooper about the way he treated me. The showdown must take place on my turf. Asserting myself in the isolation of the farm was too risky.

Despite my overwhelming hunger for Cooper's love and approval, I could no longer put up with his need to control, his incessant criticism, silences, and tantrums. I was always on guard, trying to avoid another misstep. If Cooper didn't stop blaming me whenever something failed to go according to his whims, I would not return to the farm.

For two weeks, I went about my routine in a heightened state of anxiety. While I did chores or watched TV, laid in bed at night, or prepared dinner, I rehearsed the delivery of my ultimatum, constantly revising my words, and trying to anticipate his reactions.

I packed my suitcase for more than the usual weekend stay in the city, including valuable pieces of jewelry, several well-worn novels, and my address book with phone numbers of close friends. Cooper loaded the car, not noticing the extra heft of my luggage. I slid into the passenger seat, fingers crossed. The dogs settled in the back.

The ride to the city was as tense my feet pushed against the floor each time Cooper braked. The sheriff didn't detect my apprehension. He planned the weekend's itinerary. "We'll grill in your backyard tonight and go to Casio's for dinner tomorrow night." I tried to concentrate on the changing season to avoid thinking about what was ahead of me. The cold weather was waning, and the sun felt warm on my face. Birds chirped, coaxing spring chicks to try their wings. Large patches of wet earth loomed where the last snows had melted.

At my house, Cooper went upstairs for his afternoon nap. It was time to tackle the first part of my mission.

Kira, the student who was living in my basement with her husband Dan, backed her yellow bug down the drive. I cleared my throat. "I'm planning a serious talk with Cooper this evening. Depending on the outcome, he might return to the farm alone. Do you and Dan have plans?"

"Dan has to study for a test. We'll be downstairs if you need us."

It was impossible to live under the same roof and not be aware of Cooper's erratic behavior. With my impending confrontation, I was relieved to have an ally close. A few weeks later Dan gave me a wooden baseball bat that he hid under my side of the bed – just in case. How could I love a man with whom I was afraid to be alone or be myself? A man who kept me in a constant state of confusion and anxiety.

At Borders the first display table, just inside the entry, was stacked with several copies of *Men Who Hate Women and the Women Who Love Them.* After waiting in the long checkout line, I tucked the paperback at the bottom of my purse. Cooper detested psychiatrists. He wanted to be the one digging up secrets.

Next, Kira and I stopped at Hy-Vee to buy the week's supply of groceries, including a half-dozen specially cut choice steaks, appeasement for the discussion to come. As Cooper and I prepared dinner, my shoulders tightened. I tried to make light conversation and keep my voice breezy. He marinated the steaks and lit the grill, while I prepared salad, baked potatoes, and garlic bread. I picked at my food; Cooper shoveled his meal down. It seemed like dinner would never end. Over coffee, I took a deep breath and said with as much strength as I could muster, "We need to talk."

His cup stopped mid-air. He looked at me curiously.

My heart raced. "Cooper, I love you with all my heart, but I never seem to please you. You don't realize how much your constant criticism hurts me. If it doesn't stop, I'm staying here." It was the first time that I had the courage to stand up to him.

Without a word, Cooper rose from his chair and slowly walked to the kitchen sink. Mechanically, I followed. He turned and faced me, staring over my head at the opposite wall, as if I wasn't there. He said flatly, "Can I take the steaks?"

I was stunned. Did he really say that? My insides turned to ice as if the blood drained to my feet. I had become accustomed to Cooper's hair-trigger temper when his demands were unmet, but this was different. His cold detachment frightened me more than his attacks ever had. I couldn't face the reality that he didn't give a damn if I returned to Woodland. I panicked. Terrified that he would leave me, my determination crumbled.

I put my hands on his muscular arms and pleaded, "Honey, most of the time we get along beautifully. But when you're angry or belittle me, I can't reason with you. Please, let's talk this over."

"What's to talk about, woman?"

I felt sick to my stomach. My fear of losing Cooper was far greater than living with his anger. I tried to put my arms around him, attempting to take back my words. He was stone cold.

After what seemed like an interminable silence, Cooper said, "Get your things! We're going back to the farm."

I breathed a huge sigh of relief. Thank God, he still wants me. I was so desperate for his love that I surrendered my self-worth. My failure to stand up for myself and my needs reaffirmed that Cooper gave the orders. I did a one-eighty and returned to my codependent role.

Grabbing the box of steaks from the freezer, he called the dogs, threw our bags into the trunk, and slid behind the wheel. He waited impatiently, honking the horn, while I turned off lights and locked the house. We rode in silence – my sentence for defiance. Cooper chain smoked, flicking his ashes out the open window, as I shivered in the opposite corner – more from nerves than the cool night air. I was so thankful that I was sitting next to him, driving back to Woodland and prayed Dr. Forward's book would provide the key to save our marriage.

When we returned to the farm, things appeared normal, at least on the surface. Cooper still referred to me as his woman, and we rekindled our romance. I wanted badly to believe that the craziness would magically disappear. I didn't understand that was impossible. He didn't want to change. Why should he? He had me right where he wanted – needy and afraid. We had returned to the "honeymoon phase," described in Dr. Forward's book. I had seen it so many times that I lost count. But how long would it last?

My friend, Sara, once told me, "There are times we must fall out of love." I wasn't ready, not even close.

When Cooper left for work, I pulled *Men Who Hate Women* from the closet where I had hidden it under my sweaters. My magnifier brought the pages to life. Highlighting key passages and writing notes in the margins engraved the message in my mind; I was a battered woman.

Dr. Forward's study of the misogynistic relationship described my husband and me:

"It is as if we've made both a spoken and an unspoken contract, or agreement, with the misogynist. The spoken agreement says: *I love you and I want to be with you*. The unspoken agreement, which comes from our deep-seated needs and fears, is far more powerful and binding. Your part in the unspoken agreement is: *My emotional security depends on your love, and to get that I will be compliant and renounce my own needs and wishes.* His part of the agreement is: *My emotional security depends on my being in total control.*"

How did I get here? How could I be so needy that I would seek a partner who was abusive?

I continued to read *Men Who Hate Women* in secret, hoping to find a solution. I felt despondent when the pages had no happy conclusion.

I refused to give up. Cooper meant too much to me. I would find a way to change him. Marital counseling might help if Cooper would go. I learned that victims are not responsible for a partner's abuse. I accepted the blame rather than arguing with him. When you hear it's your fault repeatedly, you begin to believe it.

I made an appointment with Dr. Phillips, a psychiatrist I had begun seeing for depression during my second marriage. We had established a trusting doctor/patient relationship. He had launched me on my journey toward self-awareness. Now I needed his wisdom more than ever. I hoped he had a blueprint for a marriage built on mutual love and respect. Janet drove me to the appointment. A small-town cowgirl, she showed up in a denim blouse, tight Wrangler jeans, and roper boots. She wore her bleached blonde hair in a low maintenance mullet. Only forty, her weathered skin revealed the hard life she had led.

I entered the spacious, earth-toned waiting room. Penny slid the glass open and smiled, "Dr. Phillips will be with you shortly."

I picked up *People* and settled on a comfortable beige couch. Glancing at the other patients, I was relieved that I didn't see a familiar face. A stigma was still attached to those who saw shrinks, implying that they are "strange" or "crazy." I caught the eyes of a young woman who looked quite normal, dressed in jeans, t-shirt, and tennis shoes with a backpack beside her;

perhaps a university student. A mother argued with a teenager who said she didn't ask to be born. I empathized, remembering horrific episodes when my children were teens. I pulled out my magnifier and immersed myself in the gossip-filled pages.

Dr. Phillips opened the door and called my name. He led the way to his immaculate office. Tall, lean, and tanned he has a runner's physique and prides himself on a healthy lifestyle – a vegetarian diet and daily exercise. A glass of water or iced tea is always within his reach. He looks like he bathes in the fountain of youth, appearing forty-five instead of sixty-something.

A well-worn Physician's Desk Reference, and a DSM-III reference book sat on top of a large custom-made oak desk in the corner of his office. On the wall between book shelves filled with psychiatric literature were several framed degrees from various colleges throughout the east.

Dr. Phillips waited for me to settle on the brown leather couch under a watercolor of lavender and white irises. He proudly said that his wife was the artist and that we could see her paintings displayed throughout the waiting room and adjacent offices. Reaching for his iced tea, he leaned back and crossed his legs – my cue to open my notebook and begin.

The counseling process is stressful. Self-scrutiny is agonizing and embarrassing. My hand shook as I started reading my notes. Although I had vented my problems to Margo, expressing them to Dr. Phillips was unsettling. He was skilled at getting to the truth. But what if I wasn't ready to face it? What if he didn't have a solution for the problems in our marriage? What if it was my fault? Dr. Phillips was my last hope. Anticipating Cooper's every need had not been enough. I felt as though I had changed into a Stepford wife: keeping my feelings and opinions to myself, smiling like a mannequin, failed to mollify him. I was tired of being the one who always gave in and got the blame when things went wrong. I looked at Dr. Phillips feeling defeated. Tears filled my eyes. "Cooper and I are having problems, and I don't understand why. There's a lot good in our marriage. We spend hours talking."

"About what?" Dr. Phillips asked.

I sat forward, "Cooper's work and case load. He knows the idiosyncrasies of the people in the county and discusses them with me. It helps me understand human behavior."

Dr. Phillips put his glass down. "You're talking about everything except what's important. You need to focus on your relationship." His voice was kind, calming.

I shifted uncomfortably. I thought communication was the most important factor in a relationship. But Cooper and I didn't have the kind of communication that would make an enduring and loving partnership. I wasn't honest with him unless I thought he'd approve of what I said.

During my counseling, it had bothered me that I bare my soul and often Dr. Phillips gives no response. I've wanted to shout, "Say something. Tell me what to do." Now he's making suggestions, and I don't like what he's saying. I want to hear that any couple who can talk non-stop on a ten-hour road trip has an enviable relationship.

He saw the desperation in my eyes. "Did you think this was going to be easy? You're willing to work on your problems. What about Cooper?"

My shoulders slumped. "Cooper acts like everything is fine. It is, as long as he gets his way."

Dr. Phillips nodded. The expression on his face remained neutral.

I continued. "Cooper has obsessions. Prisoners raped some guards in a riot at Ohio State Prison last summer. He won't stop talking about it. He's afraid of going to the Big House."

"That fear could protect you."

I was too consumed with trying to save my marriage to absorb his wisdom. I wanted the doctor to do the hard work of figuring out a remedy for our problems.

I looked at Dr. Phillips wanting to say, "Gaze into your crystal ball."

He read my mind. "If you don't do it yourself, it won't have staying power. I can provide tools, but you must do the labor."

Although Dr. Phillips always sought the truth, he never pushed me. Those of us who have been in abusive relationships know the severe ramifications of emotional dependency. Relying on Cooper and others had kept me insecure and from finding out who I was.

Dr. Phillips said, "We only grow through ownership of our decisions."

Throughout my life, I have avoided making decisions whenever possible. If the outcome was unfavorable, I could point fingers at others. I lacked the confidence to trust my instincts.

At the end of fifty minutes, he stood – my signal to depart. I was irritated by his rigid schedule. It was difficult to flip that switch. I was more disheartened than ever. The optimism I'd felt upon walking into his office had dissipated. I had been banking on Dr. Phillips writing a prescription to make my marriage work, but there was no pill to cure Cooper's volatile behavior or my dependency on him. Dr. Phillips couldn't perform a miracle.

Janet and I slid into her rusted Bronco. The carpet of green grass and smells of spring were fresh and invigorating, but my mind was not on the foliage. I was at a dead end; it was an emotional cul-de-sac. The therapy session was no panacea. I was desperate. There must be something else I could do.

Only the hum of the engine interrupted the silence as we drove through downtown Woodland. Ten minutes until we reached the farm and I turned back into a "stepped-on" wife, pretending I didn't have a care in the world. Cooper would be home from his shift and all must be fine.

Arriving at the farm, we eased onto the gravel drive. Cooper was standing in front of the barn repairing a broken hinge. He was fuming. Cursing. I panicked. In my haste to be ready when Janet arrived that morning, I must have forgotten something. My mind raced. Did I let the stove die out, leave the kitchen light on, or forget to lock the door? I don't know why I didn't think he was mad at the hinge. I braced myself. The three of us unloaded the groceries onto the sidewalk in silence. I thanked Janet, and she headed home.

Before her car was out of sight, Cooper's eyes bore into mine.

"You drove right past me this morning when you went through town. I told you your vision is getting worse."

Again, another dig at my eyesight.

Just as I had been conditioned to do all my life, I stifled my hurt and anger. I picked up a bag and climbed the steps to the kitchen. Tears burned my eyes. Cooper carried in the rest of the groceries. I avoided looking at him. I didn't want him to see the pain on my face, nor did I want to see the hostility on his. I heard the backdoor slam. Through the kitchen window, I watched him walk to the barn. He grabbed his tools and went back to work. Cooper thrived on anger. Neither Dr. Forward nor Dr. Phillips could help us. I was out of options.

Sixteen

Cooper's eyes glowed with pleasure when he unwrapped the gift that I gave him for his birthday – a pricey TAG Heuer watch. To a sheriff, it was as good as newly found evidence. "This will look great in or out of uniform," he beamed, admiring it on his thick wrist.

The impulse to indulge my husband with extravagant gifts on special occasions gave me a high. I was very particular about choosing the perfect style for a rugged outdoorsman, and I was pleased with my selection. I thought of the watch as love speaking to him every time he needed the hour, minute, or date. After my purchase, I could hardly wait until the big day. He would know how much I loved him, and he'd love me even more.

And it certainly seemed like he did. He wore that watch every day, all day, except if he was working in the field, with the cattle, or on a vehicle. Then he'd place it carefully in its box on top of his dresser right next to his badge.

A few months later, Cooper and I were shopping for a friend's wedding gift at Borsheims Jewelry, a division of Berkshire Hathaway. The store's elegance and price tags rival Rodeo Drive. A vigilant security guard assesses each customer as they enter through etched glass doors trimmed with gold. Shimmering display cases show off every precious gemstone known to man. Their custom-made jewelry is a special feature. A gift department stocked with fine china, crystal, silver, and trendy accent pieces glitter for appreciative eyes. Crystal chandeliers with designer bulbs are suspended from high ceilings. Antique, decorative Ming vases filled with eucalyptus and exotic flowers contribute to the ambiance. It's wonderful. It's extravagant. It's addictive.

Patrons are lured by a unique inventory and the opportunity to trade their own jewelry. Though there is a sales staff eager to please, the majority of customers want to be pampered by Syd, the one-of-a-kind proprietor – a showman who knows every piece in the store – its worth and yours. Syd had perfected a flashy Vegas style, and was a genius at his craft. His charisma and attentiveness made each customer feel like family. To those with money he bestowed preferential treatment, and other shoppers would cast envious glances your way. While a saleswoman helped me select a gift from the bridal registry, Cooper, in contrast to my chic designer jeans with heels, wore his typical off-duty attire: faded flannel shirt, Levis and cowboy boots. He browsed the men's watches. The salesman asked if he was a Rolex man.

"Yes," he said bending over the glass for a closer look. "I'd like to try that one on." He pointed to a diamond encrusted watch in the case, leaving his fat finger print. The salesman clasped it on Coop's wrist, and he sauntered over to me, looking like a ranch hand who had found the winning lottery ticket. He flashed his wrist and said, "Babe, I'm going to exchange my TAG Heuer for this." *That* was a prohibitively expensive *Presidential* Rolex boasting a price tag over eight thousand dollars! I wanted to scream, "No! Hell no! What's wrong with the watch I just bought you?"

He held his arm out, marveling at the diamonds set in 18 karat gold. "How's it look, Babe?"

His expression and body language challenged me to say anything but, "It's stunning." I felt like he had just kicked me in the stomach. When and where did Cooper think he was going to wear this flashy timepiece?

"I can't wait to show Michael and Jake," Cooper said. "They'll shit a brick. Thanks, Babe, you're the best!" Before I could say another word, he turned to the salesman and said, "I'll wear it."

Cooper had me on the spot. Syd knew I was paying the tab. I felt humiliated. I was far more afraid that my husband would leave me if I didn't buy what he lusted after than I was concerned about appearances or my shrinking billfold. Cooper was taking advantage like an overgrown brat in a FAO Schwarz toy store; not averse to making a scene to get his way. I reluctantly charged the watch – for better or for worse, till bankruptcy do us part. Cooper knew what he wanted and who would buy it. I wasn't ready to face the fact that I was merely a blank check to him. Being too narcissistic to care gave him a lot of power over a woman who cared too much.

The Borsheims incident was a ploy to program his little ATM to pay without question. The real power play began on a hot, humid day the following summer. It was the start of a beautiful day. We rode down country roads in his Lincoln Town car. The sky had a smoky tint, making it easier for me to see. Fields of corn higher than a man's head waved in a gentle breeze as we passed. Freshly mowed hay-scented the air. Cattle grazed in lush green pastures. It felt as if we were in a rural Midwest painting.

Cooper said, "You should purchase land near the farm to enlarge our holdings."

Why would I want to buy farmland? I was a city woman who jumped on stools at the sight of mice. Besides, his net worth had grown to a respectable amount since we had been together; yet it was *my* money that he felt entitled to spend on his dirt empire; or anything else.

"What could be a better investment?" He answered his own question. "No one can take it away. We can gaze at its beauty, sift the soil through our fingers, feed cattle, plant crops, and reap the benefits. Stocks are a gamble. One bad day in the market and where's your money? Gone!"

Alarm bells rang in my head. The agricultural world was so foreign to me; it might as well have been in China, or on the moon, for all I cared. My investments had provided the children and me with a comfortable lifestyle after their father died. But Cooper measured my love by how willing I was to pick up the tab. He didn't want a silver fork. He wanted South Fork. But how had we gotten to the point, whereby his logic, my stocks were *his* to divert to the purchase of *our* holdings? Cooper construed my silence on this occasion as compliance. He began to search for the land of his dreams.

Maybe someday Coop would come to realize that profitable stocks came on the market daily, and the investor need not break her back by cultivating soil that was subject to freak storms, floods, fungi infestations, and drought that could wipe out a season's hard labor overnight.

Occasionally, he yanked me away to evaluate a piece of property. I saw only soil, rife with weeds, thistles, and poisonous sumac. The fields he showed me were never up to his standards. However, he was undaunted in his enthusiasm to turn my assets into tillable acreage.

What would I do if, or when, he found his dream dirt? Refusal to buy him his land would end my marriage. I couldn't tell him no; my world revolved around him. Fortunately, there were long lapses between our real estate shopping trips. It seemed that anyone who had property worth a look-see was not about to part with it.

Seventeen

The TV anchor announced, "A chilling story just in; Joseph Ryan Brewster, 42, has been arrested for allegedly assaulting his live-in girlfriend, Trina Davis, 37. She is in critical condition at the Nebraska Medical Center after sustaining severe head injuries."

Cooper sat in his captain's chair cleaning his nails with a pocketknife. I stared at the mug shot of the batterer: a bearded man with long unkempt hair and bushy eyebrows, who gazed back blankly like the buck mounted on the wall. I turned away. "I don't have it that bad," I thought. "Cooper doesn't beat me."

He lit a Lucky and exhaled a ring of smoke. That was my cue to sit up and listen attentively, like a good student. "Babe, my brother Grant's been beating his women since his first hard-on. Any excuse: drunk, stoned, sober, or just because."

"Angie too?" I asked wide-eyed.

Cooper ignored my question. "Grant's pissed away more money than I'll ever see. He worked for Wisner Pipeline for twelve years, 150 grand a year plus expenses. He blew it on coke and young, hot women that he knocked around till they left."

Cooper had no reason to beat me. He had perfected verbal abuse.

I shook my head. "What a waste."

Coop took a long drag on his cigarette, the tip glowing red. "I might cuss a woman, but I'd never lay a hand on one. That's landed many a guy in the Big House. You know what happens to cops who end up there?"

"You told me," I said, careful not to sound irritated.

"Cops and perverts are at the bottom of the food chain. The queers see them as fresh meat. I don't want to be the girlfriend of Bubba in cell block eight."

Exactly what I had told Dr. Phillips.

Cooper intimidated residents of Marshall County but would bring a smirk to a hardened lifer.

He knew I was terrified of guns. They had never been a part of my life. My dad wasn't a hunter nor was he a gun enthusiast. The only weapon I wanted to see was fastened safely inside the sheriff's holster.

He liked to show off his expert gun skills. "Watch this, Babe." He stood in front of the full-length mirror hanging inside his closet door, perfecting a quick draw, and twirling his pistol, mocking the blowing of smoke from the muzzle like his idol, John Wayne.

I had never pulled a trigger and had no intention of doing so. With my limited vision, I was afraid that I'd accidentally kill an innocent person. When making the bed, I never touched the pistol under Cooper's pillow, as if it was a venomous snake.

"One of these days, you are going to have to suck it up and learn how to shoot," Cooper said. "In my line of work, I've made enemies. I want you to be able to protect yourself and me, if necessary. Someday you'll thank me."

I pictured my foot with a bullet in it.

When Cooper and I were dating, he convinced me to purchase a shotgun. "It'll save your life if anybody ever breaks in." After Boots had died, I considered owning a gun to protect the children and myself. My brother-in-law cautioned, "With your vision, you might hit one of the kids!"

Cooper brushed aside my objections and went off to procure a .20 gauge with my money, claiming it was for my protection. He placed it on the top shelf in my closet. I never touched it.

The gun was equivalent to buying me a power tool. When I moved to the farm, he cleared a place for it in his cabinet. I had no key to the case, nor did I want one.

On a chilly March afternoon, the sun reflected off the windows blindingly. As Cooper poured his coffee, he said, "You're having a shooting lesson today."

Afraid to tell him "NO" directly because of the wrath that would come down on me, I carefully chose my words and said, "You know I've never handled a gun. I'm afraid of them."

He gritted his teeth. "I'm an expert sharp-shooter. I'll show you. You're having a lesson, whether you want to or not!"

He strode to his gun cabinet in the dining room. I heard the key in the lock. The door hit the wall. His tread in the hallway sounded like the approach of the Grim Reaper. He returned with a bulky pistol in his hand. "Get up."

I froze.

He grabbed my arm and dragged me out the back door like a misbehaving dog on a leash. My ankle twisted as he yanked me down the steps; arms were flailing, trying to get a grip on the railing. I lost a shoe. He wouldn't let me retrieve it. I begged him to stop. He ignored my pleas.

"You're hurting me."

"Things are going to change around here," he yelled. "This is not your plush nest in the city. You get some leather in your attitude, or you won't survive."

I looked at his parked truck with yearning eyes, wishing I could escape. Why was he demanding that I learn to shoot a gun when it was so unnecessary? He was already armed. Why not put me behind the wheel of his tractor?

In the backyard, he jerked me toward him. His stale coffee breath and the smell of cigarettes turned my stomach. "This farm is a self-sufficient fortress. When necessary, we back everything with deadly force."

"You protect the fortress." My voice broke. "I'm not going to shoot a gun!" I was hysterical.

He shoved me. Refusal was not an option. "Pay attention!" he ordered.

Tears further blurred my world. I wanted to break away and run into the house, but I couldn't out-run him. He grabbed my head and twisted it, forcing me to look into the jet-black barrel of the gun. Hollow point bullets threatened to end my life. I squeezed my eyes shut before I could picture the deadly scene of carnage it could do.

"This is a six-shooter," he said. He opened the chamber, showing that it contained six rounds. He forced the weapon into my hands, positioning my index finger through the trigger guard and onto the trigger. It felt heavy, cold, and evil. Alien. The sweet smell of gun oil reminded me of Campho-Phenique. He used my thumb to cock it and ordered me to fire. "Just point the gun straight ahead and pull back on the trigger!"

The more he instructed, the more hysterical I became. "What if I shoot someone by accident?" I sobbed, begging him to take it back.

"There's no such thing as an accident when you know your weapon," he barked. "It's power in your hands. Learn to love it." The fear and loathing that coursed through my blood created cramps and tremors in my fingers. His revered piece fell to the earth with a ghastly thud. His face contorted with a look of pure hatred.

He slapped me on the left side of my face with such force that my head spun. He followed with a backhand to my other cheek. The weight of his hand slammed me onto the rocky ground. My body landed on sharp stones that dug into my flesh. He was bringing out my survivalist instincts all right – fight or flight. I wanted to flee. I didn't try to get up, afraid he'd push me back down. He made no move to help. I flinched as his hand passed my field of vision to retrieve his treasured firearm. He stroked the blue steel with his handkerchief. This time I didn't need my eyes to see clearly; like the steaks, he valued his gun more than his wife.

Cooper's face was full of rage as he stormed toward the house, leaving me weeping on the cold hard ground. My cheeks burned; I could barely breathe. The back door banged shut. A cold north wind traversed the countryside, rattling tree limbs and blowing dust and crop debris into my face and snagging in my hair. I laid there for a few minutes praying that nothing was broken and tried to figure out what had provoked his fury. What had I done to deserve this? Surely, he didn't mean it.

When he told me to get out of his car on that dark, scary night in Yellowstone National Park, I obeyed, thinking that he wouldn't really leave me. He loved me too much to risk my falling off the cliff into the river. I was right that time. We ended in the lodge on a king-size bed enthralled in passionate sex. Will today have the same happy conclusion?

We'd been caught up in cycles of fighting and making up, but now his violence had turned deadly. How in my right mind could I justify having a gun pointed at my head? What kind of person would pray every day that she could stay in such a hell hole? Why was I always so forgiving? How could I still love him? I forced my aching body up, bruised and scraped but not severely injured, and hobbled toward the house, scared about the greeting I would get. Would he lock me out? Would he keep yelling at me? Would he slap me again? Would he wrap his arms around me and say, "I'm sorry Babe; I didn't mean to hurt you?"

Eighteen

Fortunately, our lives had been relatively calm these past weeks. No more talk of guns or violence or revenge.

Dressing for the Annual Fire and Rescue Banquet, I paused. Holding a tube of lipstick, I looked in the mirror, past my reflection, and deep into myself. What is the matter with me? How can I love him? He pointed a loaded gun at my head and hours later expected me to make love. Even more disturbing, I obeyed. I had no choice, remembering the night he held me down on his bed and violated me following my D&C. I relived that nightmare all over again. I was thankful for the pitch-black room; it concealed the fear and contempt in my eyes at his sick perversion and my lack of the courage to stand up for myself.

I was no stranger to Cooper's emotional abuse. However, he had never hit me before. My heart raced as I struggled to breathe when he threatened to leave me stranded on a country road in the Badlands. I was afraid when he became belligerent over runny eggs, cold coffee, or wasted well water. Now I had experienced Cooper's physical violence, and I was afraid for my life.

Cooper's dark confidences had always kept me on edge. Shortly after his first marriage to Karen at age 20, he and his bride moved to Wyoming. His mother followed, renting a house near the newlyweds. According to Cooper, Nell was determined to break up their marriage and instigated trouble between the young couple.

When he repeated his tale, he'd barge into my personal space, his mouth inches from mine. I could feel his hot breath on my neck. Infuriated by Nell's meddling, his face turned red, and the veins in his neck bulged as he recounted how he had wanted to push her off a cliff. I cringed. I couldn't believe that he harbored so much hatred toward his mother. Now that there was continuous tension between us, I could see myself being hurled over a bridge into the frigid Platte River, screaming as I hit the water and rocks below.

Nell succeeded in gaining her daughter-in-law's trust. The marriage started to unravel. Angered by his mother's interference, Coop moved his wife and son to Woodland, where his grandparents had once owned a grocery store. He and Grant had spent many summers helping at the store. Nell again followed and resided permanently in her childhood home.

Coop claimed he had lived everywhere, done everything, and seen it all. Nell poked holes in his tales by refusing to give credence to his lies. I didn't want to admit that my husband was a liar. I can tolerate many human flaws but never dishonesty. Still, to protect myself from his wrath I, too, had become a liar. The image of Trina Davis was seared in my mind.

I had entered marriage with Cooper dreaming of writing our *Love Story*, based on our adventures of romantic moonlight horseback rides, with a picnic of champagne and cheese at the picnic table, accompanied by candlelight. We only rode the horse together once and never had a candlelight dinner unless the restaurant set the table. The reality was his temper was explosive, and I often withstood the worst of underserved hostility.

Diane was worried. Despite a public speaking background, I had lost my ability to complete sentences.

"Mom, when Gomer (Diane's favorite nickname for Cooper), is not around you're relaxed and open. If he's in the same room, though, you become anxious and stumble over your words. Every time you bring up a subject or answer a question you look to him for approval. You can say whatever you want."

"No, I can't. Cooper will yell at me and put me down if my opinion differs from his. I can't bear him being mad at me."

Diane shook her head. What she said was, "Mom, you've lost your spirit." What she thought was 'He's sucking the life right out of you.'

In the months to come, she became cold, detached. Before I realized what was happening, we had drifted apart. All that mattered to me was Coop: our life; our happiness; our memories; his needs; my peace.

Was I that transparent? Who else had noticed my insatiable need for Cooper's approval? I hadn't even admitted it to myself. How far had I fallen?

I knew I should leave, yet I kept praying that divine intervention would reveal a way for our marriage to survive. What if being alone was harder to suffer through than his temper? While contemplating what to do, I had to keep our lives as normal as possible.

I shook off my negative thoughts, applied lipstick at the bathroom mirror and checked my face – no bruises from his backyard assault. I was relieved. I wouldn't have to lie about walking into a door. I never dreamed I would become a battered woman. Dressed in one of Cooper's favorite outfits, a white wool pantsuit, and hot pink turtleneck, I leaned forward and wiped my index finger across my teeth.

"Let's go," Cooper yelled.

I took a deep breath and exited the bathroom. I grabbed my white clutch purse from the dresser, knocking over the change dish. Not wanting to keep Cooper waiting, I thought, "I'll pick the coins up later." He was in the kitchen and whistled when he saw me. "You clean up good, woman; you'll knock 'am dead."

I blushed, a sucker for his well-timed compliment.

When we arrived at the Fire Hall, Michael was parking his car. Margo leaned out the window and waved. Coop backed into the narrow space alongside. He always said, "Head your horses home," which this time meant parking his well-cared-for pickup too close to a big, ill-used Silverado with reinforced bumper.

"What if that man wants to leave?" I said.

"Well, he better be careful of my truck. I'm the sheriff!"

I rolled my eyes. Sheriff to him meant diplomatic immunity. I looked over my shoulder as we walked into the hall. Cooper took my elbow, guiding so a stranger would not suspect I couldn't see – or mistake me for a single woman. The four of us joined Kenny, a good man, and sheriff of the next county and his wife, Mary Beth. We had shared heaping plates of barbecue with them several times, and Mary Beth had visited me at the farm, accompanying me on a walk.

One of Cooper's deputies, Jake, arrived with his live-in, Jolene. According to town gossip, after ten years and numerous trips to the emergency room, his wife, Ann, had fled with their two sons.

Following Jake's separation from Ann, he joined us for dinner at the farm several times. One night after he left, Cooper said, "Jake and Jolene are talking about moving in together."

"Is he ready to commit to one woman?"

"No question, he's crazy about Jolene. He'd never step out on her, just like I wouldn't step out on you."

I sat next to Kenny, and Mary Beth was on his right. Cooper got up to socialize in the chow line. Kenny had taken an interest in published works of true crime cases. His recent favorite author was Ann Rule, a former Seattle policewoman. He knew I loved reading and thought I might like to pick up the book. Kenny was involved with her account of Ted Bundy, one of the most prolific serial killers in America. In her paperback, *The Stranger Beside Me*, Ann chronicles the investigation, arrest, trial, and conviction when Bundy confessed to killing at least thirty-six young women from coast to coast. I planned to buy the book on our next trip to the city. The banquet festivities broke up at 11:00. The evening had been fun. I was no longer an outcast; the townspeople had accepted me.

Outside, in the dark parking lot, we found the bed of the truck side-swiped – Silverado bumper prints on the panel. The owner of the gnarly truck left when he wanted. Under the neon street light, Cooper removed contact information that he found beneath the windshield wiper.

"I swear I'll fix that bastard," Cooper growled.

His mood grew uglier as we drove home. I assumed it was the fender bender, but when we walked into the kitchen, Cooper unleashed his rage. He stood with his back to the sink and his eyes locked on mine; he yelled, "Kenny was undressing you with his eyes and you liked it!"

My jaw dropped. Why would Cooper accuse me of flirting with another man? I had enough problems with him. Why would I invite double trouble? "That is ridiculous. I'm not interested in him, and he certainly isn't interested in me."

"I know the difference between a compliment and a come-on. My observations hold up in courts of law."

I got blamed again; it was an indictment based on his paranoia. At the beginning of our relationship, his possessiveness made me feel protected and cherished. Now it felt claustrophobic. I tried to reason with him, but his mind was made up – I was involved in a steamy, illicit sexual relationship with Kenny. For twenty-five minutes, I had to listen to his tirade. The walls were closing in around me.

Something inside me snapped. I was fed up. We had not built our relationship on love and trust! No matter how much I loved Cooper, I had to prepare to leave – I could no longer live like this. Instinct told me he had to think my departure was *his* idea. Otherwise, it would be very difficult to pull off a safe escape.

Along with his badge, farm, an arsenal of weapons, and classic cars, my "hanging off his arm" was a boost to Cooper's over-inflated ego. If I looked like a cover girl, he was proud. Time for a reverse makeover. I started chipping away at the Morgan Fairchild image he had of me. My designer jeans and silk blouses remained in the closet. Out came the baggy gray sweats and worn out tennis shoes. I didn't change after daily walks; dust covered my cuffs. I let my svelte figure go soft and pudgy. I quit taking the time to apply makeup unless I was going out in public. He missed the cute and perky Carol Brady with pink frosted lips and false eyelashes. I morphed into plain Alice.

Cooper made sarcastic remarks. "You look like a bag lady. We're headed to breakfast, not to till the garden."

In addition to my modified outward appearance, I made a subtle behavioral change. I didn't let him get under my skin when he erupted. I still walked on eggshells, but if a few broke, I could function. For a compliant woman, this was progress.

Then, for a time, things would be relatively smooth. Cooper would be attentive, loving, and kind; keeping me in a holding pattern. My need to go kept wavering. It was one thing to contemplate leaving, but another to walk out the door.

One frigid December noon Margo picked me up. We went to her house for a "girl chat" lunch. Since moving to the farm, we used the phone mainly for non-confidential conversation. On the days we couldn't wait to vent, we spoke in code because we feared a wiretap on our lines. Cooper was Snow White; Michael, Dial Tone (he worked for the phone company), and Jake, Gold.

The day before our lunch date I called Margo, "Snow accused his wife and Matt Dillon of making eyes at each other."

"Does he think she has a death wish?" she asked sarcastically.

After club sandwiches, Margo said, "I must show you my new carpet." She turned on all the lights and opened the blinds in the master bedroom, hoping my eyes could capture some color.

The trees shaded the windows so that I couldn't tell the exact shade of blue, but it felt thick and plush under my feet. "Margo, it's beautiful."

"I love it. Next year we'll replace the living and dining room carpets."

"I don't think I'll be here. I'm making plans to leave. *Don't* tell anyone, especially Michael."

Margo paused. "That doesn't surprise me. We wondered how much longer you'd put up with him." She stared at the carpet and said, "I'm not that happy either, but what do I have to return to? At least you have your home."

I looked at her. "It's an empty house."

Margo's words echoed. What did I have to go back to other than a house full of memories: sitting in front of a romantic fire holding hands as the snow fell softly outside, talking all night, and falling in love? I recalled the days he depicted life in detail so what my eyes couldn't see my mind would, Sunday brunches at Jenny's off the beaten path, sitting in a secluded booth with his arm around me, drinking endless cups of coffee from our over-attentive waitress who had a crush on Cooper. He had planted the bed of multicolored tulips to border my front porch and transplanted a beautiful maple tree from the farm to replace the diseased Dutch elm in my front yard. We'd taken exhilarating rides on his Gold Wing, the pretend Harley, and me perched on the back with the wind blowing in my face, my scarf flapping. I felt like a rebel, having traded lace for leather.

I was unaccustomed to living a hard, fast existence, but I loved Cooper and the spontaneity of our life. I didn't want to miss the next adventure. The thought of leaving was unbearable. I prayed the whole gun episode and his delusions that I was flirting with Kenny were behind us. It would take more than being slapped around to get the blinders off my eyes. My survival instincts were not yet sufficient to put my feet out the door.

Nineteen

Cooper sat in his rocker watching a western flick. I looked at the screen; John Wayne starring in *The Cowboys*. We had watched this movie together several times.

He should have been born fifty years earlier, roaming the range with John Wayne and Gary Cooper; back when a man's word and a handshake meant something. They settled problems with a fist fight at the saloon or a shootout in the street at high noon.

"May I interrupt?" I asked, fearing some resistance, remembering the last time I interrupted.

"I suppose," he said curtly, pushing the mute button, and crossing his arms over his chest. He looked at me with his 'What now?' expression.

I sat down facing him, gathering my courage. "I think we should try marriage counseling. Dr. Phillips recommends it." Our marriage desperately needs it, I thought.

"If anyone needs a shrink it certainly isn't me." He said this as if I suggested we start a family.

"It might help us. You've met Dr. Phillips."

It was a brief introduction; the two of them shook hands, and their eyes met. Their meeting certainly was not long enough for either one of them to form an opinion. Dr. Phillips' tight schedule prevented any socializing when Coop dropped me off for appointments, which I'm sure suited him; a therapist would see through his "good cop" persona.

"That doesn't mean I need to go under his microscope. I couldn't wear the badge if I didn't pass a psychological exam and a background check."

"Cooper, this is about you and me." You being too critical of me. Me living in fear of you.

"I'm fine," He said, lighting a cigarette. "All five commissioners endorsed my campaign for re-election. Would they have supported me if they thought I was a psycho?"

Turning up the volume, he directed his attention back to his movie: Wil Anderson driving his cattle herd across the prairie mentoring a group of young school boys. Conversation ended.

I sighed. For months, I had turned myself inside out trying to save our marriage, and all Cooper talked about were his accomplishments. Nothing was working. If anything, we were growing further apart.

I agonized over our future. I must make what feels like an impossible decision. For our marriage to survive, I forfeit my identity. If the marriage ends, I won't survive.

Verbal abuse had escalated to physical abuse. How much more could I take? My rational side said, "Leave." My emotional side countered, "Leave the love of your life? Are you crazy?"

The following afternoon when Cooper returned from work, he was full of juicy gossip about people I didn't know. I sat at the dining room table with him while he ate a roast beef sandwich and rambled on. Finally, he said, "Wake me in an hour-and-a-half. I have to feed the cattle before dark."

After he'd closed the bedroom door, I headed out for a walk, turning left at the end of the gravel drive. When I moved to the farm, Cooper warned, "Never hang a right. That crazy old farmer will run you over. No one will know who did it." The sounds of grasshoppers popping through the grass and the smell of newly turned earth greeted me. As always, traffic on the road was sparse. Niki and Duchess zigzagged ahead, wagging their tails, and sniffing for prey, scaring a rabbit, and chasing it deep into the field.

Ordinarily, I enjoyed the solitude of the countryside but today, remembering a recent conversation with Granny, I felt uneasy. Last weekend while Cooper and I were in town running errands, we stopped at her double-wide trailer to pick up a jar of homemade strawberry jam. Her husband, Glen, asked Cooper to come outside to see his new fishing gear. Coop always had to duck his head to go in and out of their tiny trailer door. By this time, he was so large, he first had to duck one, then the other broad shoulder to fit his large frame through.

As soon as the screen closed, Granny turned to me and said, "I worry about you alone at the farm."

I had never feared the isolation. Cooper's badge and arsenal gave me a feeling of security. The doors were always locked unless he was home. What was Granny trying to tell me? Was she concerned about my poor eyesight; that the remoteness of the farm was conducive to a break in, or was she afraid that Cooper might hurt me? Granny had lived in Woodland all her life and knew his family well. Why didn't I ask? Was I afraid of her answer?

I made a right at the intersection and walked to the brick house at the top of the hill: the fields and trees and sky all blurred together. I retraced my steps, focusing on the gravel road. The sighted take in the beauty of nature; my vision prohibits this privilege. I pondered my future. Enduring the barrage of put-downs and Cooper's recent assault with the gun brought me to walk a fine line between love and hate. In the brilliant sunshine of this spring day, I began to fantasize scenarios of his untimely demise: another high-speed chase, an oversized piece of steak lodged in his throat or a fatal shooting.

There's a knock at the door. I open it to see Sarge's ashen face.

"Sarge, what's the matter?"

"You better sit down."

"What's happened? You're scaring me. Where's Cooper?"

"He was so brave. He interrupted a robbery at the pawnshop. The S.O.B. shot Coop in the chest before he had a chance to draw his gun. He died instantly."

"No! Cooper can't be dead!" I burst into tears.

"Michael and Margo are on their way. If there is anything Bear's team can do, let us know."

What made me picture such a violent way for my husband to lose his life, I was not ready to face.

I shook off my daydream as I approached the farmhouse. It didn't feel like *my* home anymore. Was it ever? It was quiet when I walked through the mudroom. I decided to take a nap on the couch in the parlor. When I awakened forty-five minutes later, I knocked on the bedroom door. "Coop, it's time to get up."

No answer.

I pushed open the door. The spread was pulled up, and the bed was empty. I looked outside to see if Cooper had started chores. The car was gone.

I rushed to the phone and called Margo.

"He hasn't stopped here." She sounded tired of the trials of Renee and Cooper.

Why would he leave without telling me? He'd never done that before. Trying to harness my anxiety, I frantically started to clean, with the dogs, my canine support team, following me from room to room. First, I attacked the kitchen, wiping down counters and cupboard doors, cleaning out the refrigerator and tossing out leftovers. Then I moved to the back hall closet and began reorganizing my cosmetics and hair products on the shelves. I ended up in the bathroom and thoroughly scrubbed the sink and tub. Night fell, black and brooding. Every few minutes I peered out the dining room window, hoping to see Coop's headlights approaching. Finally, at midnight, I heard a car coming up the drive. Cooper walked in with an attitude that dared me to say anything. Niki and Duchess disappeared; they were nowhere in sight. "You're still here?" he said, "I thought you'd be gone."

I was so relieved to see him that I ignored his shocking words. "Where were you? I've been worried sick."

"Playing cards at Jake's."

"Why didn't you call me?"

He shrugged. "I'm a big boy."

He started his bath water. When he came to bed, I wanted him to hold me and tell me that everything was fine with us, that he loved me. Unlike other nights, he kept his distance. Soon his breathing grew deep and regular. Tossing and turning, I replayed the day's events. I had no reason to doubt that he was at Jake's. Why did he say he thought I'd be gone? That evening - was never mentioned again.

Several days later, Cooper left the truck running and rushed into the house wearing a lottery winner's smile. "Woman, grab your jacket. I've had my eye on a perfect piece of property. It's for sale! I was so excited when I saw the sign that I almost drove off the road. Let's go before someone snatches it up."

A wave of panic washed over me, sending my blood pressure through the roof. Sweat beaded my forehead. Cooper intended to add to his 160 acres until he amassed a wealth of property – with my money. I had a sick, dull ache in my heart. As he turned the truck around, he said, "You're going to be thrilled." His look dared me to disagree.

I first realized that Cooper dreamed of becoming a millionaire landowner one morning while we were having breakfast at the Sweet Shoppe. He nudged me, "See that guy parking the battered pickup?" I strained to see through the window. "That's Bart Buchanan." A man in faded overalls and a grease-stained work shirt entered the café. "Looks like he doesn't have change for a cup of coffee? Wrong. Owen Tapp says he's worth two million on paper. He made his money farming."

I shook my head. "Work shirts can be deceiving."

Cooper was an opportunist. What better funds to tap than mine? That day was the one I had been dreading since he started dropping broad hints about his real estate obsession. In the past, we had driven by farm property for sale, but he had always found fault, "Not enough acres to plant crops," or "Not flat enough." But his failure to find what he wanted never stopped him from trying to make his dream come true. He knew that prime land would become available eventually, and he had every intention of having me foot the bill.

"Every landowner I know has held on to his investment. The stock market is a gamble. Land has a guaranteed return," he repeated, trying to convince me.

My idea of prosperity was not tractors and plows and pollen-sneezing air. "The sun is blinding. I forgot my sunglasses."

Cooper exhaled a heavy sigh of exasperation, "You're not going to need them. We'll be back in a few minutes. You know how long I've been searching for the right acreage."

Fear like I'd never known engulfed me. I was clammy and felt like I was going to throw up.

I knew nothing about agricultural investments. The extent of my farming experience was four years of viewing the changing seasons from the kitchen window. Stocks and bonds have been my livelihood. While not Suze Orman, I've studied the market and made some profitable investment decisions. A diversified portfolio has enabled me to maintain a consistently comfortable lifestyle since I have been on my own.

We arrived at the "rich, fertile soil." Coop parked the truck, opened the gate, and stepped onto the property like he already owned it; his big western boots kicked up dust. He waved his arms expansively, "This is it." I followed him, shielding my eyes, struggling to see. What he saw as the potential to add more zeroes to his net worth, I saw as dirt clods and dry, cracked earth that would choke my investments. The ground was unplanted, devoid of a house or outbuildings, without trees to soften the view. I strained to see a profitable return. For him, it's a win-win. He gets what he wants, and I pay. If the crops don't yield, I still pay.

"This is exactly what I've been looking for." Looking at me over his shoulder, I heard an enthusiastic "Don't you love it? Next summer the corn tassels will be waving in the breeze. We'll cash in on a bumper crop."

Or weeds. My heart beat so hard against my rib cage, I wondered if Cooper could hear it. "It looks good," I lied, putting off my decision for as long as possible.

As we drove home, Coop was already planning his farming future. He said excitedly, "I'll need a hired man, probably Delbert, to work the fields. Call the real estate agent and get the information."

I didn't dare open my mouth but wanted to say, 'You call. You know how to use a phone.' Cooper parked. I followed him up the uneven concrete steps. As he unlocked the door, he handed me a piece of paper on which he had scribbled the realtor's name and phone number. "You better call now. It's 4:30." I did what I was told, praying there wasn't anyone there; then I'd have the weekend to think of a good excuse. But I'd also have the weekend to hear over and over and, "Let's drive by! Let's drive by!" A receptionist answered. My heart dropped. "May I talk to Ted Prettyman?" When he picked up, Cooper, still on a high, coached. "Tell him it's one mile south of Highway 51."

The realtor quoted an excessive amount of money. I thanked him and replaced the receiver.

"Damn it! Why didn't you make an appointment?" Cooper screamed. A single droplet of sweat rolled down my spine. I'm in turmoil. A positive answer ensured the continuation of our marriage – but for how long? Until my well ran dry? What would I have left? Cooper had robbed me of everything. My self-esteem was at an all-time low. He alienated my family and weaseled his way between Margo and me. He attacked my religion. Worst of all, recently he stooped so low when he belittled my deceased father. The only thing I had left was a financial safety net. I vacillated. How long could I afford to be a blank check in the hands of the aspiring land baron?

It was finally clear to me that the purchase would be for *Cooper's* benefit, not *ours*. His continued demands on my financial assets made me fear that my prayers for his genuine love would never be answered.

Timidly I told him, "I can't."

He spat out his rage, "Then get out! This is not your home any longer!"

His words stung more than the time he had slapped me in the face. I pleaded with him to change his mind. Was saving our marriage worth losing my money? Perhaps I was selfish?

"Pack your shit! We're finished. Don't take anything of mine and don't forget your precious checkbook."

I felt cornered. I panicked but couldn't say the magic words, "I'll buy the land." My fear of losing Cooper dominated any rational thought. For one desperate moment, I reconsidered my words and said, "Give me some time to think about it."

"What's to think about, woman?" His eyes were blazing red with self-righteous fury.

With my last shred of dignity, I prepared to leave. There was no offer to drive me. I didn't ask. I couldn't bear the thought of Cooper abandoning me at my empty house. He had left me there too many times. I called Janet who was visiting her mother in a nearby town. "I can be there in an hour," she said. I dragged my suitcase from under the bed and packed my most valuable possessions and whatever clothes fit in the suitcase, sobbing the entire time. How could he do this?

I had finally taken a stand, but at what price? I wanted to take back my "no." I've never felt so close to God. I'm certain He guided me. I know that had I given in, things would have been serene between Cooper and me until he wanted my money for more land or a high-priced combine to harvest his crop.

While I waited for Janet, I made myself a tuna sandwich because we hadn't prepared dinner and there was no food at my house. My fuming husband watched me eat in silence.

When Janet arrived, she put my bags in her Bronco. Niki bolted onto the back seat. She was going home! Her canine instinct was saying, this is it – bright lights, big city, no more putting up with the ogre. I climbed in Janet's car and fastened my seatbelt; tears streamed down my face. I will always see Cooper standing on the back stoop. The porch light glowed behind his head, illuminating his huge silhouette: arms crossed, knees locked, feet spread apart. I'll never forget the expression on his face. Except for a smirk, he was devoid of emotion.

Janet put the car in drive. I turned one last time. Cooper was still staring at me. Will history repeat itself? Will he come to get me when he calms down? I cried all the way home.

Part Three

Twenty

It was drizzling when Janet parked her car in my driveway. My despair mirrored the cold, dismal weather. The porch lights glared coldly, in contrast to inside lights which gave an illusion of cheery warmth. I unlocked the door; Niki raced to the couch – home sweet home. But I felt dead inside. The long, mournful faces belonged to Janet and me. Since hiring her, I had tried to keep my marital problems from seeping into our business relationship, but she was too sharp to miss the obvious. One afternoon, as we drove back to Woodland from the city, she said, "People in town like you." Her unspoken words were that they tolerated Cooper because he was the law. If a piece of expensive farm equipment went missing, you wanted the sheriff to track it down and bring the criminal to justice. When a Main Street shop was burglarized, his presence guaranteed it did not happen a second time.

"Can I carry your suitcases to your room?" Janet asked.

Afraid to speak, I shook my head. I didn't want to start crying again.

Before closing the door, she said, "Call if you need anything." I appreciated her kindness.

Like tsunami debris, I had been washed up on the shore of my former paradise. But I was too devastated to appreciate it. I felt chilled and yearned for the warmth of the wood stove, Cooper's arms wrapped around me: a crackling fire blanketing us with heat when the thermometer plummeted below zero and a blustery north wind blew trees and power lines to the ground.

My home, once my refuge, felt large, cold, and empty. Like an abandoned school yard, it was far too quiet. I could hear echoes of our former life; passionate laughter, hearty meals, and midnight *tête–à–tête*. Thank God, I'd kept it. Where would I have gone if I had sold it? I couldn't call on Margo. How could she balance a friendship between the four of us and her professional alliance with the sheriff? Diane would have welcomed me, but my nerves were on edge, and I needed a quiet room to think, which I wouldn't find at her house with three young children.

As I dragged my suitcases up the stairs, Niki scampered ahead and plopped in her spot on the bed. I ached for Cooper to be holding me, whispering how much he loved me, gripping the remote at arm's length and surfing the channels for a western flick. I was afraid that I would never see him again. We had no reason for contact – no children together, no property, and only a few friends in common. For four years, I'd poured my heart into a romantic dream. I deluded myself into believing that my husband loved me. I blocked out any signs that said otherwise, refusing to see the truth.

My head assured me that I'd done the right thing. My heart said I should have bought the land. I wouldn't be alone in this cold bed.

I felt abandoned and desperate, unable to drive to a friend's house for a shoulder to cry on. Ma Bell was my solace. I checked the time, six p.m.; four on the West Coast. I called Sara at home in Los Angeles.

"Cooper threw me out," I sobbed. The words caught in my throat like they had a will of their own and refused to come out.

Sara must have felt it was déjà vu for the umpteenth time. During the past ten months, I had shared my tug of war: I'm leaving; I'm staying. My call did not surprise her, only the way the drama had played out.

"What happened this time? Did you cut the pizza into four pieces when he only wanted two?"

I heard the whistle of a teakettle in the background. Sara was making green tea.

I told her about his real estate pursuit.

"He has money. Why does he need yours?"

"He doesn't have enough to finance all the property he wants."

"Does he want to own the whole county? Why is he obsessed with dirt?"

"It would elevate his status. I should have given him the money. We'd still be together."

"Are you insane? You'd be together, but you'd be broke. Good riddance." Her opinion of Cooper was not likely to soften at the unspoken suggestion that if I loved him so much, there must be something good in him.

I hung up, more despondent than ever.

Struggling through tears, I dialed Tammy in Scottsdale for a second opinion. She was nursing her newborn daughter. Fatigue was in every syllable of her greeting, but I didn't care. The baby at her breast made small sounds of pleasure. I shared the past painful hours and how alone I felt.

"You're lucky to be out of there," she said.

I didn't want to hear I was lucky.

"But he has a good side." Hot tears burned my cheeks as I pulled more Kleenex from the box.

She didn't respond. She had already heard my justifications for wanting to save my marriage.

Seeking consolation was the primary reason for my calls, but I also hoped my friends would support my return. They not only didn't encourage me, but they also didn't agree. Sara and Tammy had heard too many unfavorable comments and complaints from me about Cooper.

Coop had begged me to come back before. There was no reason the cycle of banishment and reconciliation couldn't play out again. Now in my depressed state of mind, I thought if we made up, perhaps I'd even buy the land.

The days passed in slow motion; still no word from Cooper. Even the most mindless activities were next to impossible: loading the dishwasher, and concentrating on a book – forget that. The only productive thing I could embark on was a walk through my neighborhood while thoughts of him consumed me; praying that he'd want me back. Every time I talked to a sympathetic person I burst into tears. I sobbed uncontrollably for thirty minutes after flowers arrived at my door from Barnhill Investment. The fragrant I-told-you-so bouquet should have evoked a wistful smile, but I was too overwhelmed with grief. I used up all my 'poor me' reserves while knowing I would run back to my man if he crooked a finger.

For what seemed like the hundredth time, I relived the hell – *"Get out! This is not your home any longer!"* At the same time, I was obsessed with figuring a way to seduce him. More than anything in my life, I had wanted our marriage to succeed. I'd put my heart and soul into it. I did everything for him. I had learned which buttons were safe to push and which to avoid. Food, sex, and gossip, as well as opening my billfold were guaranteed positives. I avoided shady details of his past. Finding fault with him or his cronies or analyzing our relationship was prohibited. After all, I thought, he is my husband in sickness and health, for better or for worse. Until death. The unpredictability of our marriage and the craziness were preferable to life without Cooper. I was as good at deceiving myself as he was of convincing me his love was genuine.

Two weeks following my return, he showed up at my door. I was overjoyed and wanted to throw my arms around him but didn't want to appear too eager. I didn't know why he was there. He brought a care package: asparagus, onions, and radishes wrapped in newspaper. No flowers or chocolates; homegrown vegetables cost nothing. But I didn't mind. I was so happy to see him. "If you're afraid I poisoned these, give them back. I don't want food to go to waste."

"Of course not," I lied.

I set the bundle on the kitchen counter to throw away later. Niki didn't sniff to see what animals Coop had been around – further proof she didn't like him.

He strode to his favorite chair in the family room. I followed, enjoying the width of his back and the scent of Stetson. I sat on the loveseat facing him, waiting for my heartfelt invitation back to the farm. We had fallen in love in this room. It felt like old times.

Suddenly, he began to cry in huge, guttural sobs. Taking a handkerchief from his pocket he wiped his eyes, "Everybody I've ever loved is gone." Thinking he meant me, I rushed over and put my arms around him. He didn't reach for me, didn't take my hand. Nothing. It was like hugging a block of wood.

"I never told you what happened to Grant and me when we were kids. One summer when we were helping at Grandpa's store, the butcher took us to buy ice cream. We headed down a deserted country road. He molested us."

"That's horrible. Did you tell your Grandpa?" All our years of intimacy and no hint of this one.

"He knew."

"What do you mean?"

His voice hardened, "Grandpa didn't want to lose his prize butcher."

I looked at Coop. He had his hands balled into fists, the veins in his large forearms bulged. His face went blank. Eyes vacant – as though he was in a hypnotic state. He looked as if he had flat-lined.

Cooper wiped his eyes again, sniffed, and stood to leave. I was sick when he didn't say, "Get your things. We're going home." Without a kiss or hug, he had gone.

Why did he stop over? How ironic. I was afraid to eat the vegetables and yet obsessed with finding a way back into his arms.

I needed an insider who would support my return. Margo was my only accomplice. She could update me on Cooper's activities. I punched in her number.

"Michael and I are sick of him," she complained. "He's been here every night since you left. We have to handle him with kid gloves, or he'll feel rejected."

"What does he do?"

"He sits at the kitchen table consuming coffee and cigarettes. He swears about you."

"What does he say?"

"You're stingy. What else? You're like a six-year-old who doesn't want to share your Halloween candy. Then the next evening he's crying because he misses you. He says you are the only woman he's ever truly loved."

That is what I want to hear. Cooper's suffering as much as I am.

"I want to come back. Will you help me?"

We planned a strategy. Perhaps Cooper's unexpected visit and his call shortly after I arrived home indicated a desire for reconciliation. "Woman, you are a class act," he had said. "You left like you do everything else, with grace and dignity."

We'd established the pattern of our pendulum-like relationship before we married. When Coop's anger reached the boiling point, his most effective punishment was to evict me. My exile usually lasted a day and night. Once he exhausted the fury and I had done penance, we could kiss and make up. He'd call, "Get your stuff together. I'm on my way." I'd quickly throw my clothes into the suitcase and wait at the door like a lonely and faithful dog. I feared separation from Cooper more than his temper. Even if he was fuming, we were together.

Ten days after throwing the vegetables away, I finally got the nerve to call and ask if I could spend the day and night at the farm. I was trying to crawl back. Coop didn't say, "Woman I love you. I need you. Come back." On the other hand, he didn't say no. There was no offer to pick me up; I caught a ride with Kira.

When I arrived, the house felt unwelcoming – smaller, like a cottage going to seed. Darker. I stretched my shoulders to relieve tension and proceeded inside, determined to make things work. I stumbled on a step – was it because of my vision or was the place already rejecting the former resident? Stepping into the kitchen was like stepping through a portal into the past: a pack of Lucky Strikes on the counter next to Mr. Coffee; the windows, where you could look out and see a small patch of the road showing through the trees surrounding his yard. Everything was the same as when I moved in.

As usual, we talked about everything except the day I told him "NO." He was a sheriff, and that meant you became adept at reading people. He didn't try his romance for finance angle. Maybe he had remembered telling me about the woman from whom he had supposedly refused to take money.

Our lovemaking, which had always been exciting and romantic, was now void of emotion. Where was the passion? Where was his sweet whispering in my ear, "You're my woman; I can't live without you." There was no deep, soulful kissing. He wanted the sex to be unforgettable, so I would know what I was missing. We reached a divine summit. But all the heat and fusion of skin left no afterglow. I felt cold and empty inside. There was no resolution. I had been alone even when in the thrall of sexual pleasure. His lovemaking was indifferent.

The next morning, we ate Cheerios and drank coffee. Very little was said. I was in the home of a stranger. He filled his cop mug, gave me a perfunctory kiss on the cheek and left. He didn't ask me to stay.

I called Margo. "It's hopeless. He doesn't want me."

She consoled, "He'll call later."

"I'm going to give him until 2:00 before I call Kira for a ride."

Hours passed. No phone call. I was in deeper despair than before. The visit to the farm was a failure. I no longer had any hope of reuniting and felt crushed. Maybe the human heart is just plain blind or stupidly hopeful. Kira drove me home.

Twenty-one

I met my friend Crystal for lunch at the mall where she was a makeup consultant for a top-line cosmetics company. She waved as she applied the final additions to a young woman's eyelids. Resembling actress Jill St. John, Crystal has flawless, radiant skin, dark, shiny shoulder length hair, a sparkling personality, and beautiful, straight, white teeth. Today she wore a new shade of pink lipstick called Apple Blossom.

After closing the sale, she smoothed my blush with her ring finger – an invasive gesture that annoyed me because I didn't see it coming. I preferred to be told about the smudge and repair it myself. But I didn't say anything because I wanted her to like me, and she was just doing her job.

While buying cosmetics, Crystal and I began a friendship that has continued through the years. She gave me tips to find the right shade of foundation for my skin tone and the correct tools to apply eye shadows and blush. In the process of picking out color palettes, I shared my separation heartbreak and horror stories, while she talked as though raising children was a honeymoon.

Crystal hung her smock on a hook, and we headed to the Peacock Room. She daintily unfolded her napkin, placing it in her lap. Although it had been thirty years since she moved from Mississippi to the Midwest, she had retained her magnolia drawl.

"Brian says we must keep our distance. Cooper is a loose cannon." It seemed she couldn't get the words out fast enough.

I choked back tears when I should have said, "No you don't get to abandon me right now in my time of need." All my life I have kept my thoughts and feelings to myself, fearing that I might alienate those about whom I care: a serious flaw; I needed not to be afraid to speak up.

What I was facing the end of my marriage. No matter how dysfunctional, I was married to the most exciting man I had ever met. I needed my friends to stick with me while I worked through my grief. Or, if my prayers were answered, we would reconcile.

"That hurts," I said looking around to see if anyone had overheard our conversation.

Seeing my tears, Crystal took my hand. "Don't worry. We'll figure something out. I think you knew early in your marriage that there were serious problems, but you were determined to make it work." She was right.

As the waitress refilled our coffee, Crystal said, "I want you to meet my friend, Iris May Waters. We're long-time neighbors and attend the same church. Her first husband was a tyrant. After she and her daughter had fled Earl's brutality, she vowed to be a guardian angel to those trapped in domestic violence. She's now happily remarried. I took the liberty of telling her about you. I hope you don't mind. She asked that I give you her number."

I called Iris May as soon as I arrived home. She invited me to lunch at her house the following week. I hoped she'd help me find a way back into Cooper's arms. My nights were long and sleepless without his comforting bulk at my side. My loneliness was unbearable. Even though Cooper verbally and financially abused me, I still loved him. I didn't think I deserved better.

The day I was to meet Iris May finally arrived. I peered impatiently out the window waiting for my new driver, Loretta. Finally, I heard the rumble of a Pontiac 6000. Barring periodic breakdowns and locking her keys in the car, Loretta and I managed to reach our destinations. I had given up my independence years earlier when I handed Mark the keys to my yellow Chevy Caprice. I had gotten in an injury-free accident at a busy intersection. Neither the driver of the pick-up nor I received a ticket. Nevertheless, the fender bender prompted me to retire from the wheel. My eyesight had worsened, and I would never forgive myself if I hurt someone.

Dr. Solomon didn't think it was necessary. "You've got a few more years left behind the wheel."

But I knew my peripheral vision had declined to the point that if a dog, a deer, or God forbid, a child darted from the side of the road, where my vision was its cloudiest, I wouldn't see them until it was too late.

Iris May's house was in a well-groomed neighborhood. Loretta's car sputtered up the driveway of an expansive brick ranch with shake shingles. The yard was freshly mowed – lush green grass with the sidewalk edges perfectly tapered. Blooming rose bushes bordered the front and pots of hot pink geraniums graced the steps. "This is beautiful," Loretta said admiringly. Iris May met me at the car. She was wearing casual navy slacks and a print cotton top. Blonde, with apple cheeks, she had a genuine smile and gave me a warm embrace; I was a sister. I began sobbing, an embarrassing and uncontrollable reaction to empathetic people I now meet. Not wanting to rush, she suggested that I give Loretta a call when we finished. Loretta waved as she backed down the driveway. With her arm around my shoulder, Iris May guided me through the front hall into the country kitchen. "I'm making tea. Would you like some?"

"That sounds good." Her hospitality was soothing, like my mother cooking oatmeal for breakfast. Iris May's appearance and mannerisms reminded me of celebrity chef Paula Deen. Her lunch preparations gave me a chance to survey the spacious room. A round oak dinette set sat in front of bay windows, where you could see an oversized silver maple, inhabited by a variety of birds and a family of squirrels. A blue braided rug under my feet and ruffled yellow pillows on the chairs made me feel like I was in a cottage. Bookshelves covered two walls. "You're a reader," I said, excited that we shared another connection. I strained to read the titles.

"I'm a compulsive buyer," Iris May said, setting placemats on the table. The tea kettle began to whistle. "Every time I go shopping, I purchase a cookbook. What you see is only part of my collection. The rest are in the basement. Marty's latest count is four thousand." She grinned, "He teases there may not be enough lumber to build adequate shelving."

I soon learned this domestic diva is very intelligent. Over tuna salad sandwiches, we shared similar, painful pasts. She poured tea; I poured out my heart, giving her a thumbnail account of my life with Cooper. "We'd have extended conversations about the townspeople, his farm, and his job. We'd talk about books and the news. He wanted me to see the things that he enjoyed, like nature, and the town expanding, a recent construction site. There was always a new adventure compared to life here alone. I feel empty."

Iris May put down her cup. "Surely, he has a volatile side?"

I couldn't deny that Cooper could be volatile. Nonetheless, I defended him, "Cooper's nit-picking was meant to help."

She looked at me incredulously, "Is that what he told you? Baloney!"

I shrugged, staring out the window.

"How long have you been married?"

"Only three years, but maybe to him that was too long."

"What caused the breakup?"

I told her about the land.

"Doesn't he have credit?"

"He always said it was more beneficial for me to invest in land rather than stocks. I would finance the investment, and he would harvest the crops, and we share the profits." As I said these words, I realized how ridiculous they sounded. I didn't even believe it myself.

I did not expect the conversation to go like this. I wanted Iris May to agree there was a lot of good about my husband and that I should return.

"He sounds a lot like my ex. Crystal probably told you about Earl?"

"She didn't go into detail."

Iris May set a plate of home-made brownies on the table. In between moist, chewy bites she explained, "We were married for eighteen years. I could never please that man. I was a regular at Willow County General. The first time, Earl broke my nose. Eventually, I limped in with a broken ankle. When a wise nurse asked how it happened, I told her the truth."

Were Iris May's physical injuries worse than my psychological wounds? "He beat you? How awful."

"Bones mend. Cruel words are never forgotten."

I ignored her comment. "Why did you stay so long?"

"We took our vows before God, and I didn't want Zoie to grow up without a father. When she became a teenager, Earl no longer thought of her as his little girl. She was a woman – the enemy. He began lashing out at her. Zoie wished I had left years earlier. She couldn't stand the way her father treated us."

"Did it take you a long time to get over him?"

"After all those years of abuse? No!"

I started to cry. "I miss Cooper all the time. I was a fool to leave." He wasn't out of my system yet. I still felt the pull back to him; like an alcoholic or drug addict. Susan Forward described this as "withdrawal symptoms," saying I needed to be clean at least six months. I still had a way to go.

Iris May said, "You know a lot more about your marriage now than you did before. You must accept that the relationship, as you saw it, never existed."

"But I'm lost without him."

Iris May said, "When you feel the pain, try to identify the cause. If you're realistic about how things really were, you will gradually begin to understand Cooper's sickness better and miss him less."

"How did you survive on your own?"

"It was very difficult at first. Earl begged me to come back. He threatened to kill himself if I didn't. I called his bluff and filed for divorce. He wanted the house, furniture, stocks, and bonds. I gave him everything he asked for, praying he would leave us alone." She shook her head, "I was terribly foolish. Nothing was ever enough. He paid minimal child support. Zoie and I moved into a small apartment with practically no furnishings. I got a secretarial job at a bank."

"How long before you met Marty?"

"He was a manager at the bank. We started dating a year after I got hired. He was also a victim of spousal abuse. We dated for three years, both of us afraid to marry again. Thank God, we did. There have been many challenges blending our families, but we've always worked them out. We love and respect each other."

Iris May and I are trying to solve my problem with different solutions. I am desperate to find a way back. She is hell-bent on keeping me out of his clutches. She is not surprised at my determination to save my marriage.

Forever the defender she put her hand on top of mine. "Don't go back. It won't get better. If you return, there will be a honeymoon phase. You know, exactly, what I'm saying. After promising you that he'll change and a bright and happy future, his cruelty will escalate. It's going to be the hardest thing you've ever done. But you don't have to do this alone. I'm here for you."

I appreciated her genuine concern, but not her advice. I looked at my watch. Three hours had passed. It seemed like only fifteen minutes. I called Loretta.

After hanging up, I asked, "What attracted you to Earl?"

"The same qualities that drew you to Cooper. Our husbands exude charm. When it shone on us, we were blinded. Don't go back. I don't want to attend your funeral."

Twenty-two

Weeks later the phone rang, interrupting the nightly news. It was Cooper! A rush of excitement surged through me. I tried to sound calm, not wanting him to know how much I missed him.

His voice was playful, "I'm not filing for divorce. I swear. It will only happen if you pull the trigger."

I breathed a huge sigh of relief. See? He does love me! I sagged against my headboard. A smile crept across my face. I looked up, "Thank you, dear God." I glanced at the clock – 10:20 p.m. – too late to call Margo. I would share my good news in the morning. Since my eviction from the farm, the nights had been agonizingly long and lonely. I was constantly wondering what Cooper was doing. Was he seeing another woman? Did they go dancing? Was she younger, prettier, without a handicap? Did they spend hours talking like we had?

The next morning, I ate a hasty breakfast and went to the phone. I didn't walk. I floated. Nothing could wipe the smile off my face.

"Hello," Margo said in her husky voice.

"Guess what?" I blurted. "Cooper called. He's not going to file."

"Are you sure?" she asked.

"Yes! He subscribes to the 'good ole boy' mentality. His word is as binding as a contract."

"I knew you would come back. It will be liberating for Michael and me. Coop still comes over every evening."

Laughing, I said, "It won't be long until he's spending his nights where he should – with me."

The doorbell rang. Who could that be at this early hour? I hope it's the new book I ordered. I excused myself. Through the glass sidelight, I saw a man in a brown uniform wearing a belted holster. It's Cooper, I thought. Smiling, I opened the door.

My face fell. The man standing on my porch was a stranger. "I'm Deputy Sheriff Martison with the Marshall County Sheriff's Department. Are you Renee M. Cowan?" He held a sheaf of papers. Official documents.

"Yes?" I nodded unnecessarily.

"You have been officially served with divorce papers by Cooper L. Cowan." The deputy handed me the summons and returned to his cruiser. Stunned, I stood motionless at the door, as he backed down the driveway. My hopes and dreams vanished. Cooper, the man I loved and trusted, had lied to me. Why?

Back inside, I threw down the packet on the counter.

Margo was still on the line when I picked up the receiver. "Cooper's a damn liar. A Deputy Sheriff just served me with divorce papers."

"What? That devious S.O.B.!" She sounded genuinely shocked.

For the first time since Margo and I had known each other, there was an awkward silence. We hung up.

I had seen my husband deceive others, but I never thought he would lie to me. Oh, how gullible could I be? It didn't take long to solve this mystery. By saying that he wouldn't file, Cooper gave me hope and then blind-sided me. He was up to his old tricks, building me up just to tear me down.

For four years, I had dedicated my life to Cooper. I had loved a lie. Like any bad habit, I had to go cold turkey to save my life. I would not allow one more betrayal; this would be his last. I felt a strength I didn't know I possessed. I had to fight, and I would prepare for that.

I needed shrewd and ruthless counsel; an attorney who could hold his own in a tough legal battle against my conniving, controlling husband. Who would know the best divorce lawyer?

My mind leaped to Jay Gold, who acquired financial security at age twenty through marriage to my sister-in-law Auddie. Since the young groom had no money, goals, or degree, my husband, Boots, and his father picked Jay up by the collar and taught him the insurance business. During the early years of his employment, he spent more time on the golf course than in the office – taking advantage of Boots and my father-in-law. They continued to coddle the fledgling for Auddie's sake. Fortunately, Jay grew into his job and got promoted to a full partnership in the firm.

Jay is a George Hamilton look-alike: very tanned, tall, medium build, with a full head of salt-and-pepper hair, and exceedingly bright.

I dialed information, and they transferred me to his office at its new location. We hadn't talked in years; not since his divorce from Auddie. He sounded pleased to hear from me. We shared significant events from our out-of-touch years and updates about our children, who were close in age.

"I'm getting a divorce," I burst like a steam pipe under too much pressure.

"I'm sorry to hear that," he sympathized. "Having gone through it myself, I know how tough it is."

Yeah, yeah. Save the obligatory condolence. "Jay, I need your help. I'm looking for a lawyer who won't be intimidated by my husband. He's in law enforcement." I would reclaim my self-respect. I'm out to win!

After a brief pause, Jay said, "Do you remember Harlan Ridgebach?"

"I know the name."

"He can't be bullied. He's someone you'll want in your corner; he's a real problem solver. Harlan will see that you land on your feet."

Harlan Ridgebach and I had never met, but the rumor through the country club grapevine was that Harlan was quite the lady's man. However, I trusted that Jay was steering me in the right direction. When he offered to look up Harlan's number, I pulled a pen and piece of paper from my desk drawer.

I called the man I hoped would take charge of my divorce and waited for him to call me back. His voice was virile, self-assured, and charming. He didn't remember me. I jogged his memory with my maiden name, which screamed old money, giving me an immediate pass on the credit check.

"My brother-in-law, Jay Gold, recommended you. I've been served with divorce papers. My husband is a county sheriff, a real shyster, and continues to prove he can't be trusted. I need a cunning attorney. Someone who can stay one step ahead of Cooper."

"You've got him. I'm not afraid of anyone." I liked Harlan's 'take no prisoner's' attitude. We set our first appointment. "Bring the summons, the divorce petition, a copy of your latest tax return and records of all financial assets and liabilities. I'll look them over, and we'll plan our strategy. Then I'll send a letter to your husband's lawyer."

I breathed a sigh of relief. Harlan Ridgebach would have my back – for a price.

I had no idea what was ahead of me.

Twenty-three

For the third time this week, the high-pitched wail of my newly installed alarm system startled me out of a deep sleep. I bolted upright. Niki yelped in alarm and crawled under my bed to escape the ear-piercing siren. It was 12:25 a.m.

The phone rang. "Are you all right, Ma'am?" the Moorehead security operator asked.

"No!" I screamed, "I think someone's in my house!" The panic in my voice said "HELP!"

"The police are on their way. What is your location in the home?"

"My bedroom upstairs!" Kira and Dan had moved out, and I was all alone. The house is sprawling. I imagined a hatchet murderer had broken in and was hiding around the corner, lying in wait.

"Stay where you are until the police arrive. Is there a lock on your bedroom door?"

"No!" I shrieked, still trembling.

"Our monitor shows the alarm was tripped at the front windows. The police will be there any minute." The operator remained calm, reasonable. Me? I was out of my mind with panic! Just stay away from the living room windows was the advice I detected in her words.

I hung up and listened for footsteps or the creak of a stair, my heart thudding in my ears. I knew the sounds of the staircase when someone was ascending or descending. Each flight had its unique creak and groaned under the weight of traffic. The house talked to me in its old age. Not hearing anything, I popped a Xanax. For peace of mind, I dialed 911.

"Yes, Ma'am," the dispatcher said. "Officers are on the way."

Unable to bear the deafening noise, I gambled that no one was on the stairs with a gun, knife, or baseball bat from my son's closet. Memories leftover from childhood returned to me. I felt my way down the steps to stop the hideous racket. Just as I pressed the correct sequence of numbers to silence the alarm, the doorbell rang. Niki and I jumped. "Who is it?" I yelled.

"Police officers, ma'am," a deep, gravelly voice of no-nonsense authority said.

I opened the door to two uniformed officers.

"I'm Sergeant Collins." A brawny guy, gray at the temples, with a well-groomed mustache, carbon-copy of actor Ed Asner, stood at my door.

"I think someone's broken into the house." I wanted to cry, partly from fatigue but mostly from relief knowing protection had arrived.

After stepping into my entry way, he introduced his partner, "This is Officer McBratney." She stood taller than Collins, was wafer-thin, and wore her shoulder-length dark hair pulled back tight in a ponytail. She nodded, scanning the rooms; much like Cooper did the first time he walked through my door. Cop mentality.

"We checked the premises. There's no sign of forced entry, but we did find boot prints in front of the bay window," Collins said.

It's HIM. A chill ran down my spine. Cooper's spying on me at night through the windows!

I knew that Cooper was responsible. Victims of domestic violence say that they instinctively sense when they are a target, and when trouble is about to escalate. A protective alarm clicks in their heads. It could be physical, like the hair standing up on the back of your neck. Or it could have been intuitive; that feeling deep inside that something just doesn't feel right. It reminded me of my friend, Roxanne. Early in her relationship, her new beau Vince became irrational. Every time they went out he thought other guys were hitting on her and she was flirting back. She felt smothered and broke up with him. He started calling, begging to see her, promising he would change. She finally gave in. Things went well for a few months. Then he accused her of having another man in her bed and threatened to blow her brains out. She knew she should never have given him a second chance.

I had no proof that Cooper was the culprit behind the terrorism other than unidentifiable boot prints.

I pulled nervously at the neckline of my robe. "Officers, please check the entire house; closets, behind curtains, and the basement. I'm legally blind. Someone could be hiding in dark corners, and I wouldn't see him."

With flashlight in hand, Collins asked if anyone lived with me or if I had any other pets. I tagged along to be certain they inspected every corner; the light beam bobbed up-and-down, back-and-forth. Not finding an intruder, they moved toward the door. Desperate to delay their departure, I said, "Would you like some coffee?" They declined.

Still trying to stall, I asked, "What kind of boots? Work boots? Motorcycle boots? Cowboy boots?"

They shrugged and shook their heads.

"Cooper, my soon-to-be-ex, has been terrorizing me."

"That's a serious accusation. Would you care to explain?"

"My property is being trashed. Many mornings, my front yard looks like the city dump. Pop, beer cans, and fast food wrappers scattered everywhere."

"It looks like your alarm system did a good job of scaring the intruder off," Collins said, trying to quell my fears.

"Please, sit down," I implored. "There's more."

We sat at the coffee table. "I'm exhausted. The alarm has been tripped at least eight times in the past two weeks."

Collins pulled a pad from his pocket.

"Could the dog have set it off?" McBratney asked.

"Niki was asleep on my bed," I said.

"Ma'am, alarm systems can malfunction. Is this one new?"

"The installation was completed five weeks ago."

As Cooper and his guns safeguarded the farm against outside threats, I had prayed the ear-piercing alarm would provide protection from *him*; never mind a random break in. When the installers completed the last circuit, I chose a code. The technician handed me the operator's manual and two panic buttons; one went on my nightstand and the other on a shelf above my kitchen desk. I hated that he'd completed the job because his presence made me feel safe.

"One morning when I went into the garage to throw out the trash, I stepped on broken glass. Someone had shattered." the window

"Have you talked to your neighbors? Has anyone seen or heard a trespasser?"

"The houses are too far apart, except the one to the north. The judge wouldn't hear anything. He drinks."

Collins nodded.

"My gates are padlocked…"

They looked at each other. "They weren't locked when we got here. The locks were on the ground."

So, whoever did that had a key.

"Not again. That is what I'm saying. I wouldn't leave my gates open. The tulips that my ex planted have been dug out, leaving craters in my yard. Two nights ago, the phone rang in the middle of the night. A female, identifying herself as a police officer said, 'Several dogs have been poisoned in your neighborhood. If you see or hear any suspicious activity, call 911 immediately.'"

Collins made a note. "We'll check on that."

"I suspect that my estranged husband's new girlfriend made the call, but I still worry about letting Niki out. I don't know if he'd poison her. I wouldn't put it past him." I glanced at her sleeping between the officers' chairs. She must be feeling cooped up. "He knows how much I love my dog. I know he's responsible for the vandalism and the phone calls."

"Did you change your locks?"

"Immediately after I moved back here: only the house. I didn't think I needed to on the gates." Maybe I should have installed additional bolts, clamps, and latches. I had better change the gate locks too.

"What is your husband's full name?"

Now I had their attention. "Cooper L. Cowan. He's the sheriff of Marshall County."

Collins' pen paused, "Describe him."

I excused myself, went upstairs to my bedroom and carefully slid Cooper's picture from under the glass on my dresser. I looked at him one last time. He reminded me of a burly lumberjack: green and white plaid flannel shirt, carrot-top hair, and massive shoulders. I took the photo downstairs and handed it to Collins.

"What kind of vehicle does he drive?"

I gave them a description of the truck, the Lincoln Town car, and the Camaro. "All are registered in Marshall County."

I had hoped the police would charge in like gangbusters and save me. It isn't that easy outside of Hollywood.

Like a telemarketer reading from a script, McBratney informed me they would place a "special attention" on my house. A cruiser would drive by and check the premises on a regular basis. "We can't do anything unless we catch someone in the act."

"By then my house could be on fire or my throat slit!"

McBratney shook her head, probably thinking I was a total nut case, which by that time, I was. I was powerless against Cooper, which scared me. I expected a little more compassion from a female officer, but McBratney was more detached than Collins. I learned another lesson – police are reactive, not proactive. I was a prisoner at the farm. Now I was a prisoner in my own home.

"We'll take one more walk around the premises and relock the gates. Don't hesitate to call if you need anything, Ma'am," Collins said.

As the cruiser's lights vanished into the night, I glanced across the street where there is a creek thick with trees and brush. Could Cooper be lurking there watching the police investigate? Chuckling to himself? Calling them rookies? Goosebumps rose on my arms. I pictured him in camouflage gear, makeup, and night vision binoculars.

A week later my doorbell rang at 9:00 p.m. I wasn't expecting anyone. "Who is it?" I called out from a safe distance, where no one could see me through the glass side lights.

"Renee, it's Nell."

I opened the door slowly to Cooper's mother, making sure she was alone and not being held at gunpoint by her son. She hugged me. "I miss you," she said. "It's lonesome at the farm without you."

"I've missed you, too, but I can't let you in. I've been having problems with Cooper. When he finds out you're here and he will, I'm afraid of what he might do to me."

"I tried to warn you," she said. "Remember how you raved about Cooper when we met? All I could say was, 'Coop is different.' I know my son."

I felt bad that I couldn't invite her in, to hear more about "her son." She understood. I closed the door behind her and set the alarm.

The harassment continued. The phone woke me in the dead of night. Once my lifeline, it was now my enemy, giving me flashbacks to Alfred Hitchcock's classic *Dial M for Murder*. When I picked up, I never said anything other than hello. One evening a man screamed in my ear at the top of his lungs. I was terrified and hung up immediately. Other times I heard only heavy breathing. I let Cooper control the length of the call, knowing they were his doing. He wouldn't stay on the line long because he was afraid of a trace. After hearing a click, I'd replace the receiver. I tried calling the number from caller I.D. A disinterested mechanical voice repeatedly said, "Your call cannot be completed as dialed. Please try again."

I changed my number, but the phone rang over and over. It's possible that Michael gave the sheriff my unlisted number. Michael was working for the telephone company at the time. I let Coop think he still had power over me. The calls were far less threatening than his appearance at my front door.

Exactly where had ignoring all the warning signs during the past four years with Cooper gotten me? Even after he held his gun to my head, I'd stayed. The fact is, my worst fear –him abandoning me – had come true long before now. I should have listened to my instincts.

Twenty-four

Loretta drove me to the office of the divorce attorney I hoped would keep Cooper in Marshall County and away from me. "Thanks, Loretta," I said, stepping out of the car. "I'll call when we finish." Arranging rides with her had its challenges. Our schedules didn't always coincide. I like to be prompt, and she was often fashionably late.

The high-rise granite building is in Regency neighborhood; a stone's throw from Borsheims Jewelry. I took the elevator to the second floor, which opened to the partner's suite of offices. Engraved on the oversized glass door was *Weylan, Weylan & Ridgebach* in gold French Script lettering. The receptionist who greeted me was young and slim with long blond hair pulled back in a French braid. She had the face of a supermodel: large blue eyes and a petite mouth. I gave her my name. She smiled, as her job required. "I'll let Mr. Ridgebach know you're here."

I looked around the reception area – cozy with a small couch and a perfectly pruned Bonsai tree in the corner. An elaborate oriental rug covered the dark, hardwood floor. I didn't have to wait long. A confident, GQ man in his early fifties walked briskly across the room to greet me; his right hand extended. He was about 5'10", athletically built, with wavy black hair and amber-colored eyes rimmed with thick, long dark lashes – women described them as bedroom eyes. Harlan was a man who knew how to use his good looks to get ahead in and outside the courtroom. We shook hands and exchanged pleasantries. He led me down a long corridor to his spacious office. We passed a conference room with an oak table in the center and volumes of law books on the shelves. A good sign. I hope he's read them all. He had paintings in handsome frames displayed on the walls. No expense spared, I thought. Extricating myself from a toxic husband would help pay for the posh furnishings and high-end designer. I followed Harlan through the doorway of his impressive office. Floor to ceiling windows overlooked the parking lot.

The first thing Harlan did was proudly point to an enlarged picture of his kindergarten class standing on the steps in front of Dundee Elementary School, my alma mater. They had just celebrated their fiftieth reunion. He was nostalgic when he identified himself as the cute, curly haired boy in the front row. His behavior seemed odd for a professional appointment. He gestured toward a striped Chippendale near the door, "Have a seat." I was surprised at how far away from me he sat. There was no chair positioned across from his desk; just a large open area. We seemed to sit miles apart. I sat on the edge of the wingback, pen in hand, notes ready. Leaning back in his swivel chair, he looked me up and down. Given his reputation, I expected that, and he lived up to it. We reminisced about family and growing up in Omaha. He did some name-dropping, mentioning a former neighbor of mine with whom he now played tennis. I relaxed.

Harlan pulled out a legal pad and began asking routine questions: when and where Cooper and I were married, our occupations, financial history, current sources of income, and what triggered the separation? Looking up from his notes, he said, "Is there a chance for reconciliation?"

Clearly, he had never met Cooper. "I desperately wanted to reconcile, but once he had me served with papers, it was out of the question."

I told Harlan about the threatening phone calls in the middle of the night and the damage to my property. "One day there was a dead mouse on my porch. I know it was one of Cooper's juvenile pranks. He knows that I'm terrified of mice. Fortunately, a friend saw the corpse and disposed of the ghastly thing before I stepped on it." I shivered. Coop carried a mental file of what he considered practical jokes. He often put a dead mouse or frog in the coffee cup of a female county employee. Intelligent, outspoken women were a threat to him, and they suffered for their assertiveness.

I expected Harlan to jump up, pump the air with his fist, and shout, "We'll stop this prankish behavior immediately!" But it didn't seem to faze him. He shuffled papers around on his desk. Hadn't he heard what I said? Feeling sorry for myself, I thought, "Have I no allies?" Harlan said matter of factly, "If you hear any suspicious noise or see anything out of the ordinary, call the police immediately."

Where was Harlan's outrage? How could he be so calm about the nightmare through which my husband was putting me? I didn't realize until later that Harlan had become desensitized. How many times had he heard similar stories from other estranged wives?

"From now on you are to have no contact with Mr. Cowan," Harlan stated emphatically. "This is what I'll need at our next appointment." I began writing.

"I'll request copies of your husband's tax returns from his attorney." He rattled off other required financial records.

Supposedly, I had the best attorney that money could buy, but I departed with some reservations. Did Harlan have the skills to protect me from Cooper?

Twenty-five

I was double-knotting my Adidas preparing for a morning walk when the phone rang.

"How's life in the big city?" Cooper asked, taunting me.

I was on guard. All the hoops I'd jumped through to keep him happy came to mind.

Harlan had warned me to have no contact with Cooper, but I was afraid if I hung up, he would kick my door in at two in the morning. He might have my house mysteriously set on fire. I pictured him straddling the kitchen stool at the farm, drinking coffee and chain smoking. He spent hours on that hard stool, talking to cops, lawyers, judges, politicians, and his hunting buddies.

"I was just leaving for a walk," I said, immediately regretting my words. Cooper did not need to know my whereabouts.

"The sun is bright. Don't forget your seeing-eye dog."

He's baiting me. Why?

"The forecast looks good for blowing the cobwebs off the Hog. You can't drive the damn thing. How about letting me keep it?"

So that's what he wants, more boy toys.

"Sure, Coop, you can have the motorcycle."

I should have taken more time to think it through.

"Great. I'll ride up in the morning, be there at 9:30. Have a cup of coffee ready, and you can sign over the title."

During our marriage, I had tried to buy his love. Now I was trying to buy my safety.

The next morning, the doorbell rang promptly at 9:30. Niki growled, the hair rising on her back and neck. Cooper, wearing a Cheshire grin and showing his fangs, stomped his cigarette out on the porch. He knew I detested cigarette butts littering my property. As he entered the foyer, his eyes cut to the security keypad by the coat closet.

"Huh, I see that you have a new protector," he said ridiculing me.

(As if he didn't know.) "You could call it that," I said.

"Bet it cost you a pretty penny."

Not as much as my last protector, I wanted to say.

He squeezed his expanding girth into the chair he had once claimed at the kitchen table, waiting for service. I poured his coffee. Ms. Accommodation. I slipped back into the enabling behavior that I was accustomed to since we met. It's hard to break a bad habit.

Cooper lit a cigarette and looked around. "You didn't waste any time getting rid of the ashtrays." I placed a saucer in front of him. I felt like a nervous little mouse darting around trying to make him comfortable so we could finish our agreement. After one cup and small talk, he handed me the title. As much as I wanted to get reimbursed for the money I contributed towards the purchase, I didn't dare ask. It was too risky.

"Here's where you sign." He put a beefy finger on the X.

I relinquished my half.

"By the way," he said folding the title and tucking it in his breast pocket, "I figured you'd be happy to get rid of the shotgun."

I feel as though I'm back on the cold hard ground at the farm. Thank God, I did not get buried under it.

I said, "I have no use for it."

After almost four years, it was finally making sense. The gun was never for my protection. Cooper wanted it for himself. Before he suggested we live together, he was testing how easily he could be manipulate me.

He stood to leave.

"Come pick up the hospital bed," I said, hoping all these peace offerings would sever all ties between us. At Cooper's request, I had purchased it to relieve the pain from his injured back. I was sick of looking at its heavy metal frame taking up space in my home.

"Michael and I will drive the truck on Tuesday and take it off your hands. Well, I have to get back in time for shift. Some of us have to work for a living." He grinned. "Thanks for the coffee."

Typical Cooper; no 'thanks' for the bike, shotgun, and bed. Of course, I had never received any gifts from him except plants that died and flowers that wilted.

Closing the door behind him, I sighed with relief. I hoped he would leave me alone, now that he had the bike, the guns, the Rolex, the bed, the coat, the steaks, etc., etc., etc.

As he rode away, so did our good times. My fondest memories included riding on our bike. I loved the adventure – the wind in my hair and the envious stares of onlookers.

Today I shudder thinking that I let him into my home when I was alone. I was a fool to ignore my attorney's warnings. In hindsight, I should have had Cooper send the title to Harlan's office. Knowing Cooper's underhanded nature, he could have slid any legal document in front of me: power of attorney, a life insurance policy, or the deed to my home, and I would not have known because I couldn't see what I was signing without my magnifier. I put my life and financial security in jeopardy when I opened my front door. The news is full of horror stories about abusive men and women who murdered their lovers after losing control. I still hadn't admitted to myself that Cooper was capable of killing me. He had many opportunities. I thank God for keeping me safe.

Several weeks later my phone rang as I was emptying the dishwasher. My spirits lifted when I heard Margo's voice. We hadn't talked since the deputy served me with divorce papers. The chips were down, and I'd never needed her friendship more.

"We need to talk." Margo's voice quivered. The panic in her tone gave me chills. Her breathing sounded as though she was hiding in a closet from a predator.

"Cooper says you must give him $50,000 by Friday. If you don't, he's going to hurt you bad. Listen to what I'm saying! He'll make you pay one way or another. Don't call your lawyer. It'll make things worse." She hung up. I heard another click before I placed the phone on the cradle. Cooper had been on her extension.

Frantic, I pushed in my guardian angel's number. "Iris May!" I screamed into the phone.

"Is he there? Should I call the police?"

"Margo just called! Cooper's demanding $50,000 by Friday."

"What? Fifty thousand? Is he crazy? You're not doing it."

"I don't have a choice," I sobbed.

"Oh, yes you do! Who does he think he is? Why did Margo make the call?"

What could the sheriff be holding over Margo's head to convince her to break the law? He must have unearthed something juicy that threatened to ruin her reputation. That's what he does best; targets a person's indiscretions and weaknesses to benefit himself. "Cooper is smart enough not to get his hands dirty. I have to give him the money."

"You're not giving him a dime."

"You don't get it, Iris May!" I shrieked. "He'll kill me, and get away with it."

Nothing could drown out Margo's warning: *He'll make you pay one way or another.* Cooper had terrorized others. Now I was the one dangling on the edge of the cliff. In the past, I had shrugged off his murder threats towards his mother and others as angry rantings. Margo's words made me a believer.

"Call your attorney," Iris May pleaded. "Let him handle this."

"I can't call Harlan! He'll insist that I ignore Cooper's blackmail. I don't want to die. There's no negotiating when he wants something." With my life hanging by a thread, it was impossible for me to think rationally.

"Please call Harlan," Iris May insisted.

Barely able to dial through tears and my uncontrollable shaking, I reached out to Evan Barnhill, my financial adviser. I wasn't calling him to get a cashier's check for fifty grand, but knowing he would calm me down and give me judicious advice.

Dear God, let him be there. Evan picked up.

Sobbing, I repeated Cooper's latest criminal demand. I was thankful that Evan didn't say, "A prenup would have protected you from this."

"Do not give him a penny!"

"You *don't* understand, Evan."

Knowing he would get nowhere with me, he said, "May I call your legal counsel?"

That's the second person to suggest this. Once again, I pictured myself looking into the barrel of Cooper's gun. I wore out the carpet pacing the floor. I had to give Cooper the money. My life depended on it.

An hour later my phone rang.

"Have you lost your mind?" Harlan shouted. "What the hell are you thinking? You're not giving Cooper Cowan one cent unless the court orders it."

"He'll kill me if I don't!"

"Call his bluff! If you give him half, he'll want the whole candy bar!"

"Of course, you can say that! He's not holding a gun to your head!"

Click! I can't believe he hung up on me!

I was so angry at Evan, Iris May, and Harlan. They didn't understand Cooper's penchant to get even. I called Diane who understood. She rushed over and put a recorder on my phone. Had that device been installed earlier, Margo and Cooper would both be sitting behind bars: Cooper for extortion, Margo as his accomplice. My daughter also gave me a can of mace. She put it on top of the grandfather clock in the entryway and said, "Carry it with you whenever you leave the house."

I was panicky. What was I going to do?

Finally, Harlan's words sank in. Cooper was not going to stop bleeding me until I was living on the street with a shopping cart full of aluminum cans. But how could I save my life and not give Cooper any money?

Despite the danger, I had to get out of the house – the walls were closing in on me. Maybe I could think more clearly if I was in the fresh air, hiking my historic neighborhood. Fairacres is home to some of the most luxurious real estate in midtown Omaha. Walking outdoors had always been therapeutic. It was a positive activity: it helped me unwind. In walking shoes and desperation, I took off at a brisk pace, ignoring the mail in the box. I was a distraught woman in the middle of a divorce, living in constant terror. I hoped the physical activity would loosen me up and invite sleep.

The shoulder of the road bordered the wide lawns in front of my home, and the residences of neighbors; no sidewalks on my side of the street. The street ascends a hill with a grammar school on the other side. It was a popular area for walking and jogging. With my limited vision, the speed limit afforded a comfortable margin for safety when traffic approached. In the air was a faint smell of water and foliage; the creek was at the bottom of the hill.

I heard the grinding of a starting car or truck behind me. There was a pelting of gravel from beneath the undercarriage as the driver put it in gear. Unconsciously, I stepped on the shoulder of the road to increase my margin of safety. Sometimes teenagers roared through the neighborhood in defiance of the speed limit.

As I reached a mass of shrubbery, the loud sound of the engine was close behind. The shoulder-height dense shrubbery in the neighbor's yard prevented me from retreating further from the road. The vehicle tires crunched gravel too close for comfort and sent an icy chill down my spine. I tried to enter the prickly brush, but its thickness made it impossible.

As the car came over the curb, a bumper grazed my leg. My heart beat loudly in my chest, adrenaline impelling me to press into the bitter scented, bristly foliage. I wanted to scream for mercy. Tears of horror splashed hot on my face.

Then it was gone, the sound of it fading into nothing. I never got a look at the beast that could have killed me, nor the driver. With gut-wrenching clarity, I knew how close serious injury or death had been. I turned back toward home, scraped and bruised, not yet thinking of how lucky I was to be able to walk. It was intentional. The day was clear. There hadn't been any on-coming traffic or witnesses at the time. There had been plenty of open pavement.

The incident made me temporarily forget the divorce and the poison sheriff to whom I'd promised myself. In the safety of my home, I called Diane. She asked, "Are you sure it wasn't the greedy S.O.B. who was trying to squeeze you for fifty K?"

I stopped breathing at the thought. Cooper was the obvious suspect if great harm came to me. He wouldn't chance it. No, not by any stretch.

Or would he?

He was an expert at cutting off people's air. No one had escaped the jail since he was elected sheriff. Now my home began to feel like a jail. Sure, I still had enough visual power to look both ways, but no one has eyes in the back of their head. The near-miss put me on high alert.

Iris May suggested that I come to her house for a brainstorming session. As we sat at her table agonizing over my crisis, I asked, "How long do you think he's been planning to harm me for more money?"

"Since you wouldn't buy him the land." She patted my shoulder, "Don't worry, we'll figure something out."

When I thought that all was hopeless, she slapped her hands on the table and said, "Write your original life insurance policy."

I looked at her like she was looney. "How?"

She devised a plan, and I went home to execute it. Sitting at my desk, I painstakingly composed a letter. Four drafts later, Diane typed it, and I had it notarized. We put it in the mail so that each addressee could receive it before the weekend. I sent a copy to Harlan Ridgebach, Evan Barnhill, and Dr. Phillips. A fourth copy went into my safe-deposit box.

The letter stated:

I'm sending this information in case I am harmed in the future. Cooper L. Cowan, Sheriff of Marshall County Nebraska, threatened me if I didn't give him $50,000.00 cash. I received this extortion demand by a messenger, Margo J. Sutherland, a Marshall County Commissioner. Furthermore, she said that if I did not give Cooper the money, he would go for my jugular, paste my finances all over the county, fill the jury with his friends, and put his farm up for collateral to obtain the $50,000.00. During our marriage, Cooper repeatedly divulged threats he'd made to others. His intention was to frighten me into handing over every penny I had.

COOPER'S THREATS TO OTHERS ARE AS FOLLOWS:

1. When Cooper was nineteen, he and his wife were in the process of buying a ranch in Wyoming from his mother. According to him, she decided not to sell. This infuriated him, and he said he thought of throwing her off a steep cliff. "You wouldn't kill your mother," I said. He answered that he had come close.

2. Cooper owned a small business in Woodland for ten years. A customer owed him money. Cooper went to Hastings, Nebraska intending to 'bust his knee caps' with a baseball bat if he did not pay the debt. If Cooper felt anyone owed him, he would collect one way or another.

3. Cooper had an affair with a married woman. She later filed for divorce. During the deposition, she broke down under questioning and

admitted to the liaison. The woman's husband threatened to sue Cooper for alienation of affection. He confronted the man outside of court and told him that he would win the suit (which amounted to approximately $20,000), but that he would not live to enjoy it. The suit was immediately dropped.

4.   During Cooper's divorce from his first wife, she claimed she had a right to some of their farmland. He told her she would probably get the land, but that she would never reap the benefits. She abandoned her plan.

5.   Cooper said that he had three "best friends" who would do anything for him. His criteria for "best friend" was described in this manner… "All I have to do is ask, and they will have a car, a gun, and a duffel bag full of cash at a designated location."

Cooper swore that if anyone "screwed him" he would seek revenge at the right time. It might take months or years, but it would be done!

If I so much as stub my little toe, Cooper L. Cowan, Sheriff of Marshall County, will be responsible.

Renee M. Cowan

When I signed my name at the bottom of the paper, I felt a weight lifted: a new kind of protection. As I proofed my "life insurance policy," I noticed that four of the five threats pertained to money.

During this turbulent time, Cooper called one day. I said, "If you have questions, call my attorney. We're getting a divorce." I was finally fighting back, and it felt good!

He was infuriated and slammed the phone in my ear.

I called Harlan and said, "Please inform Cooper's counsel that if he doesn't leave me alone, I will get a restraining order." Harlan concluded his letter to Mr. Norris, "If we go to divorce court, we will demand remuneration because Renee had assumed the lion's share of expenses during the marriage."

I remained on guard but felt more secure now that three influential people were aware of Cooper's threats. I had a blade to attack his Achilles heel and prayed his fear of the Big House would keep me alive. He had taught me to exploit the enemy's fears and weaknesses. I had graduated from boot camp.

Twenty-six

On her way home from work, Diane stopped to see if I was still alive. When she was a tiny golden-haired four-year-old, she had said, "When I grow up, I'm going to live next door." Recently she and her husband had purchased a house as close as they could afford; in a young, friendly neighborhood one mile away.

We carried our pop to the breakfast nook, located at the center of the house. Since my banishment from the farm, this is the room where I feel secure, and you will always find me sitting at the head of the table. With my back to the wall, I write my life story, listen to the news, favorite books on CD, talk on the phone, and can hear what's going on in every area of the house. And, of course, I eat. Built-in corner shelves at each end of the table display family heirlooms. My favorites are two colorful, ceramic, French, antique jugs with male cartoon faces. As a child, I found their expressions scary. When I was growing up, the jugs' appearance became humorous and a topic of conversation. They survived the boat trip which my mother's family made from Russia, worlds away from the kitchen at the farm where a handgun occupied the windowsill and muddy cowboy boots stood at the back door.

Sipping Dr. Pepper, I complained, "I'm so sick of waking up to trash in my yard every morning and the police officers' indifference when they're dispatched here after the alarm goes off."

Diane crossed her legs Indian-style. "You can't expect them to camp out in your driveway."

"I feel trapped. I'm afraid to be home alone, and yet, I'm terrified to leave the house."

"Well, you felt safe when you stayed with us. Pack some things and…"

"Thanks, Honey, but I should be able to sleep in my own bed."

During this unnerving time, I had stayed at her and her husband's house for a few days. The kid's commotion, however, soon made me miss my home.

"You're always welcome." She looked over her shoulder at the wall clock. "I better go. I told the sitter I'd be home at 4:00."

As we stepped outside into the warm sunshine, she suddenly grabbed my arm, pulled me back inside, and called Niki, as if there was a sniper in the trees across the street.

"What's wrong?" I asked, trying to look past her to the creek.

"Speak of the devil. There he goes with his cowboy hat over his horns."

"Cooper?" I said, shocked.

"Sheriff Stalker, who else? He's cruising your block in the Lincoln. A woman is practically sitting on his lap."

"What does she look like?" I was jealous. Had he upgraded? Or had he done worse?

"Blonde hair yanked up in a ponytail, moll-style."

"Is she prettier than me?"

"Of course not. The woman's a total skank."

I sank into a living room chair, feeling depressed. Dammit, he's already got another woman?

Diane peered out the window. Satisfied that Cooper had not stopped, she paced. "There's no reason for him to be in your neighborhood. You need to take precautions."

"What more can I do? I've done everything but dig a moat and call my Italian connections."

She called her sitter. "I'll be late." Uneasy that Cooper would drive by her house, she warned, "Keep the kids inside."

We grabbed another pop. Maybe it should have been vodka tonics.

"Mom, I'm worried. What if I hadn't been here and you started down the driveway to take your walk? Who knows what he would've done."

I pictured myself sprawled out on my front lawn.

"I'm calling a private investigator," Diane said, flipping through the yellow pages. "You need an extra pair of eyes. If Gomer's vandalizing your yard, we need to catch him in the act."

I knew I had to do something, but call a P.I.? Wasn't that a bit extreme? And costly?

"Let's call a few agencies and check their fees; you lose nothing by making contact."

On Starr caught her eye. The firm was located eight blocks from my home. Diane left a message. Starr Allen called back, and we made an appointment.

The following afternoon the doorbell rang at 1:00. I was confused when I opened the door. I was expecting a seasoned detective from Hawaii Five-O, not a Barbara Eden clone. Starr was a bubbly, diminutive, blonde in her late thirties. She was wearing a hot pink t-shirt, tight fitting jeans, and plaid tennis shoes. After handing me a business card pulled from an oversized purse that looked more like luggage than an accessory, she introduced her husband. "This is Andrew. He's an attorney," she bragged. He mumbled a disgruntled, "Hello." Starr probably twisted his arm to accompany her. She leaned down to pet Niki, who was wiggling around at her ankles, tail wagging furiously. Talking fast and non-stop, she looked up at Diane, who stood behind me like a bodyguard.

"You're beautiful. Do you model?"

"I've done a little, but not professionally," Diane replied, fluffing her hair self-consciously.

"I also work part time for Dundee Modeling Agency," Starr said. "I teach a class on applying makeup every Wednesday night. I'll set up an appointment for you to meet the owner. Danielle and I are like sisters. She's been in the modeling business for twenty years. Your makeup and hair look perfect. Who does your hair?"

"I do it myself," Diane said. "I'm a cosmetologist."

"So am I," Starr exclaimed. "What a coincidence! We have so much in common. I work three days a week at The Rumor Mill. My clients want to look ten years younger when they walk out the door."

Diane smiled. "Don't we all?"

My beautiful daughter has received accolades since she was a baby, and I'm very proud of her, but why couldn't Starr focus on *this* job? I wanted to scream, "You're here to keep me safe, not to recruit models." I herded everyone to the living room, and we sat around the coffee table. Diane served soft drinks.

"Starr chugs a six-pack of Coke daily." Andrew smiled fondly at his wife. "It gives her boundless energy."

Now we're a soda pop commercial. So that's Starr's secret, I thought. Caffeine. "What are your fees?" I asked, trying to hurry things along.

"We'll get to that in a minute," Starr said, sipping her Coke. From her gigantic bag, she pulled a worn notebook and said, "Your husband is sheriff of what county?"

I told her.

Andrew interrupted, "Do you mind my asking, who is your attorney?"

Ambulance chaser, Diane's look said.

When I answered, Andrew said, "I know Harlan. He's one of the best."

"Have you changed your locks?" Starr asked, finally concentrating on the case at hand.

"Yes."

"We know an investigator/locksmith, Derek Vodika. He lives near Woodland. I could ask if he can dig up dirt on your husband."

"You can't!" I shrieked, startling everyone. "Cooper knows Derek." It doesn't make any difference if they all think I'm paranoid. I have a right to be.

"Did your husband ever hit you?" Starr asked.

The gun incident drew Starr's undivided attention. She frowned. "My friend is in a shelter. Her husband beat her so severely that she landed in the hospital."

"Starr," I said impatiently, "I'm sorry to hear about your friend, but let's work on my problem."

"We'll make a trip to Woodland to do surveillance. Somebody with Cooper's background might be involved in illegal activity."

"No! He'll find out and kill me!"

Starr shrugged. "I understand. We'll go to Plan B. My partner, Sam Burnam, will stay at your house at night. Nothing scares him. Let's try it for a week. He'll be here at 8:00 tomorrow night. Open the garage door, so that he can drive right in. He'll leave each morning at 6:00." She gave me the charge for body-guarding.

I gasped.

Starr reeled me back in. "I own two dogs, a Rottweiler named Michelob and a German shepherd, Pilgrim. I'll send over whichever one you want. Sam will protect you inside. If the dog starts barking, let him out. He'll fence in any intruder." She rattled off the additional charges. I grimaced at the high price of safety.

She continued, "I've been breeding and showing Rotts and shepherds for fifteen years. I teach an obedience class twice weekly."

Andrew added, "Starr is a notary public in case you need something notarized."

My heart sank. Jack-of-all-trades, master of none. I took my magnifier out of my pocket to look at her business card. Could all these occupations be listed on one little 2" x 3 ½" card?

Concerned that Starr was spreading herself too thin, I considered returning to the yellow pages. That would have meant rehashing the Cooper hell. I chose to stay with On Starr.

Sam Burnam reported for duty the following evening. My vigilant daughter arrived early to help lock up my jewelry. In retrospect, it was crazy. I hired a detective to guard the house, and I was hiding my valuables?

Diane opened the garage door. A Raymond Burr look-alike entered. He stood 6'4", was built like a linebacker, and weighed at least 300 pounds. He towered over us, proud of his ability to intimidate. He wore a white polo shirt, blue jeans, and tennis shoes; all probably purchased at the Big and Tall Man store. He carried a huge bucket of chicken, three liters of Pepsi, and a pillow, which looked like a Chiclet under his massive arm. After introductions, Sam, a no-nonsense kind of guy, made room for his chicken and put his pop away. The fridge groaned. Still clutching his pillow, he was ready to start body-guarding. Diane gave me her let-Cooper-mess-with-this-bruiser look.

I didn't know which man I feared more, my bodyguard, who was walking from room to room, peering out the windows, eating an extra crispy drumstick, or the one I suspected was lurking in the ravine across the street. Sam's silence was eerie. He didn't speak unless spoken to and then only in terse phrases.

I thought I was buying rest but lay staring at the ceiling counting the dollars I was burning instead of sheep. Meanwhile, downstairs, Sam Burnam flipped through copies of Sports Illustrated magazines between his rounds of the house. The neighborhood was quiet. The nights passed without incident, as if a crow whispered in Cooper's ear, "Stay away." Had he been tipped off? Was he spying from the brush in the park across the street? It's the perfect hiding place because the creek bank is overgrown with mulberry trees, cottonwoods, and nettles. Police have made occasional arrests for stabbings and muggings: upscale neighborhoods are no longer immune to crime.

Hiring Sam gave me a reprieve from my fear of being beaten, shot, or having my house destroyed. Later in the week, he developed a crush on Diane. When he began paying too much attention, I stepped in. "Not on my nickel," I said.

Starr was fun but flighty. Not only her appearance, but her personality disproved the stereotype of a hard-boiled detective. She was anything but – gullible, impulsive, and vulnerable, and yet she was a P.I. who did her job well. With a generous heart, she would give her last dollar to a con. She thought with her heart, not her head. It was bizarre and costly but provided comic relief during a grim period in my life.

Twenty-seven

Collins and McBratney had just left after the call center of my security company dispatched them again. For what seemed like the hundredth time we had to go through a tiresome search of my home and property. By now they knew their way around. Again, we came up empty handed.

Once my heart rate had slowed, I called Gail. We hadn't talked for a while, and I missed her. After a grueling two and half years of required and elected courses, she had received her Master's degree in business from the University of Oklahoma. She had accepted a job at a bank in Houston. For the first time, Gail expressed her worries about Cooper.

"I never trusted him. He always had to be the center of attention. He just wanted money, and I was afraid he might hurt you to get it."

"You saw that too?"

"Mom, everybody could see the dollar signs in his eyes. I'm so relieved that you're back home and safe."

After hanging up, I pulled the business card that Collins had given me from the pocket of my robe:

Women's Center for Advancement – Omaha Nebraska

WCA stay safe grow strong
24/7 Crisis Hotline
402-345-7273

I called.

The counselor who answered introduced herself cheerfully, "I'm Dottie." Even at this desperate hour, she patiently listened while I poured out my fears about my ex. The mind games that Cooper subjected me to were familiar to her. She assured me that as far as marrying Cooper, well, we all make mistakes. That didn't help me much, but her comment about my safety did. She said Cooper was probably bluffing with his threat of bodily harm because he knows the law. I agreed that he didn't want to jeopardize his job and that his biggest fear was going to prison.

The Hotline became my safety net in the middle of the night. There was no emergency the next time I called; I just wanted to talk. Heather made a recommendation, "We offer domestic violence education classes for victims. It's a safe place to discuss your personal experience. You might consider the program. It gives you an opportunity to interact with others in the same situation."

"I don't think I'm ready to open up about my life with Cooper." I was ashamed and embarrassed. How did *I* get into such a mess? I was a college graduate. I came from a stable background; grew up in a good neighborhood. If I talked about it, that would make the abuse real. I was trying to get past my last four years, not stay stuck in them. Cooper had stripped away what little confidence I had. Even the simplest decisions, like what coffee cup to drink from, had become overwhelming. I was still afraid of him. I could see him lurking in the shadows, gloating at each new hurdle he put in my path.

After Boots' death, I spoke at church gatherings for widows. I invited Vera, an acquaintance whose husband had recently died, to be my guest. "No thanks," she said, "one of me is enough." As I considered the violence prevention program, her words resonated. Hearing about the abuse of others might make me even more depressed. But having participated in group therapy and women's support groups myself, I found them constructive and comforting and decided to give the sessions a try. If they weren't beneficial or became too upsetting, I could do what I had always done – quit. Several days later, I called the WCA, located in midtown. The receptionist said that Mary Frances, the head facilitator, would conduct an interview to see if I met the required criteria. We made an appointment.

I was nervous as Loretta and I parked at the one-story brick building. What am I getting myself into? How could I explain that I stayed in a bipolar relationship for four years because I thought I couldn't live without my husband?

At eleven o'clock, Mary Frances strode purposefully in my direction. Her approach reminded me of Miss Clavel in the children's book *Madeline*. I recoiled, feeling vulnerable and threatened. An ostrich of a woman, she was fiftyish, tall, and bone-thin, with a pointy beak-like nose and sharp jaw. Her short gray hair had a hint of red. She wore a white blouse buttoned up the front, a black, calf-length, A-line skirt, and black oxfords, reminiscent of her earlier years as a nun.

"Renee Cowan," she said. Her authoritative voice and brusque manner sounded like Cooper when he was in one of his moods. I was trying to avoid this was the type of person, but Mary Frances was the one to approve my admission to the class. We entered a small office that was in disarray, with files and papers strewn on the brown metal desk. Pointing to a chair across from her, Mary Frances sat down, put on her wire-rimmed glasses, and started to hand me several sheets of paper.

"I'm legally blind," I said apologetically, as though it was my fault.

"Then I'll read the questions," she replied, wasting no time.

The questions were those I've had to answer too many times. Some were general, others, more personal, but I never felt they were intrusive.

"Did your husband read pornographic magazines or watch X-rated videos?"

"He was an avid watcher of the Playboy channel."

She nodded. "When your husband was angry at you, did he withhold sex?"

"That was my only break from his nightly demands." I smiled. Mary Frances did not.

"Did he use drugs or alcohol?"

"He drank an occasional beer and had an unending supply of Flexeril and Darvocet prescribed by his doctor for his back pain."

She made a note and looked at me over the rim of her glasses. "Did your husband harm animals?"

"He yelled at his dog Duchess and kicked her when she didn't mind. Her hunting days were over; she was of no use to him. I felt sorry for her. During our last year together, my dog wouldn't go near him or get into his car unless I got in first." I told Mary Frances about the strays he brought home: a black lab and a terrier mix. "After I bonded with them, they mysteriously disappeared."

When Mary Frances had heard the whole sordid story, she said, "Are you prepared to admit in class that you were abused?"

I answered, "Yes." Denial was no longer in my vocabulary.

On the following Monday, the reception area at the center filled with women who looked as desperate as I felt. I wondered if they would all be in my group. They were probably just as curious.

At 6:55, our "Miss Clavel" led twelve women to a dimly lit room; smaller than I expected. Couches and chairs arranged around the perimeter, with a few end tables holding tall lamps that gave an opaque, circular glow. We settled in chairs which became "ours." The women were all ages; some single, some married, and others, like me, in the process of getting a divorce. A few trying to decide if they should leave.

Mary Frances and Abby, the co-facilitator, took chairs by the door, a dry-erase board hanging on the wall behind them. We, the victims, each gave brief summaries of the misery that brought us together.

I expressed the emotions I felt at the hands of the man I thought was my true love. There were times that he made me feel cherished and protected. Even when things were going well, I was afraid that I would say or do something that would trigger his short fuse, and he'd become enraged. When he did, I felt humiliated, lost, and panicky.

In the presence of the other women, I suddenly became self-conscious and analyzed each word I had uttered. Did I say something foolish or offensive? Would they like me? Here they were again: my self-doubt and fear of rejection.

On the surface, it looked as though life had been good to me. Most of the women didn't earn in two weeks what I had spent on my outfit. If I had thought about the disparity, I would not have worn Calvin Klein jeans and my good jewelry. I was grateful for my financial security but too consumed with the drama in my life and the process of healing to think about the message it might convey. I left my precious stones at home for the remainder of the meetings.

I was no different than the other participants. It didn't matter what we looked like or talked like; we were all in the same leaky lifeboat, struggling to build new identities. It reminded me that women who share deep feelings in a group form a bond that promotes hope and healing.

That night as I readied for bed, I didn't feel so alone. I had revealed my obsession for a man who had the potential to kill me, and I heard similar horror stories.

Early on Bev, Rachel, and I gravitated toward one another and began a custom of stopping for coffee and pie after the meetings. We continued to vent in an informal surrounding, where we could laugh and poke fun at each other as well as ourselves.

Bev, a forty-something mother of four, was married to an FBI agent. She was working on the courage to file for divorce. Her 5'6" frame was concave. High-strung, she swung her leg back and forth in a fidgety manner the entire two hours. Devastated by the possibility that her husband had molested their fifteen-year-old daughter, she had much to concern her. Another cop, I thought.

Rachel, who was younger still, was insightful, open, and deep. She is one of the most loyal friends I have ever had the pleasure of knowing. Our friendship has lasted through the years. Her infectious sense of humor made us all laugh. She had escaped her hot-headed husband by running to a shelter in the middle of the night with her two daughters, aged three and four. At one of our early meetings, she had the group in hysterics as she imitated her husband, Frank, sounding like a third-grade bully. In our fragile state, the laughter was healing. She always offered sarcasm leavened with humor to lighten the mood. She is the only person I know who can turn an everyday occurrence, like making a peanut butter and jelly sandwich, into a comedy routine.

One evening a young woman came to the group in tears. Her face had bruises, and her left eye was swollen shut. She had a fresh cut on her upper lip. "My boyfriend beat me," Jenna said through tears, keeping her head down, trying to hide her injuries behind her long hair. "I spent last night alone in the emergency room. I had to lie about what happened because I'm afraid to file charges."

Rachel spoke up, "Maybe I don't have it so bad. Frank never beat me." A few women nodded.

Mary Frances stood up, clenched her fists, and said angrily, "Wrong! Abuse is abuse is abuse – no matter what form! Whether it's physical, verbal, sexual, or financial, we must recognize abuse when it happens, confront it, and never let it destroy us."

Unfortunately, we didn't see Jenna again. We all hoped that she had gotten away.

Shortly after we started the sessions, Mary Frances asked, "How many of you saw red flags early in your relationship and chose to ignore them?" Several hands shot up. Others were gradually raised to make it unanimous.

"It's important that we take these warning signs very seriously. Trust your instincts. If something makes you feel uncomfortable, run, don't walk away." Mary Frances encouraged us with widespread arms, "Ask for what you want 100% of the time. You may not get it, but it never hurts to ask."

Later Rachel said, "Mary Frances saved my life. She gave me the courage not to return to Frank."

She saved us all.

My need for help was as legitimate as the others, but as the meetings progressed, I sensed that Mary Frances resented me. Although it was unspoken, I think she saw me as an interloper. What kind of problems could a woman have if she can pay her bills and still have a few dollars at the end of the month? But domestic violence is not limited to any socioeconomic or ethnic group. We shopped in different stores, but it had nothing to do with how we felt on the inside or how we were treated.

The program comprised three levels of sessions. After completing the second, Abby suggested that I sign up for the third.

"I've gained so much," I said, "and will always be grateful to each of you for what I've learned. Now I need someone I can talk to on a deeper level. Someone who shares the "abuse" connection with me because of her unique experience. Although the people are very nice and understanding when I call the hotline, I never know who's going to answer the phone. I need to see my growth outside that I feel on the inside. If Cooper pulls something on Tuesday, I don't want to wait until the following Monday night for support."

When I began calling Rachel, I was impatiently waiting for my divorce to be final. She was attempting, once more, to see if her marriage was salvageable. She soon decided it was not. Although we were compatible in the group, I had no idea if a friendship would grow. I wanted an ally to whom I could pour out my heart; someone who would respect my confidences and never judge. My tried-and-true friends knew the Renee I was trying to break free of being: insecure and always trying to fit in. Rachel and I were two broken spirits reinventing ourselves. It would be a long time before I trusted anyone except Diane, Iris May, and Rachel. At times, I would let self-doubt cripple me. When nothing seemed to go right, I vented my frustration to perceptive Diane and levelheaded Rachel, whose sarcasm drips with honesty. At low points, I would phone them, especially when I had to figure a way to get to an appointment or meeting. "I never should have left Cooper," I sobbed to Rachel one day.

"No, we did the right thing. We're miserable, but at least we're not heavily sedated sitting on the floor in the corner of a padded room wearing straitjackets."

Our friendship continued to evolve to a deeper level. Rachel said we were like water and oil; extra pounds were her handicap, while mine was visual. Her children were starting grade school; mine were out of the house. My dad was white collar; hers was blue. She was employed, I was not. She is Catholic; I am Jewish. She is the first one to throw a party; I'm the last one to go.

The bond between us would not have survived if our only link was a history of being emotional punching bags. We're never embarrassed to tell each other how we feel. She always understands.

One evening as Bev, Rachel, and I left the building, Abby approached and asked how we were doing. Bev answered, "I've had a bad day." She related an uncomfortable incident.

"I bet you focus more on the negative than the positive," Abby said.

Her comment hit home. I struggle with the same proclivity. Even though Cooper had put me through hell, I had a lot for which to be thankful. I had my home, my health, a supportive family, and great friends. The women against violence group provided the tools I needed to begin the formidable task of putting my life back together.

Twenty-eight

On a peaceful Indian summer afternoon, I took a minute to make a tearful entry in my journal. Writing my feelings was therapeutic: a way of coping with and overcoming the heartbreak of losing Cooper and a second failed marriage. One minute I could be crying over him, the next cursing him. The air was dry and hazy; a better eye day for me, with a warm southern breeze. Typical unpredictable Nebraska weather: the furnace ran yesterday morning to take the chill out of the air, and today the air conditioner was keeping the house comfortable in the lower seventies. The phone rang. I wiped my tears as I picked up.

A rare call from Harlan. "Cooper's attorney has scheduled a deposition in Woodland."

"What's a deposition?" I asked nervously. "I didn't have one in my divorce from Donald."

"Donald was a cad, not a crook," Harlan said matter-of-factly. "Since we are unable to reach a financial agreement with Cooper, this is his revenge. We made a reasonable offer where each party would walk away from the marriage with the assets in his or her possession, and pay their individual legal fees. Cooper rejected that offer, so I, in turn, made a demand that he pays you $20,000; half of his increased net worth since his marriage to you. Also, I demanded $17,000 to reimburse you for gifts that you bought him, plus my fees since June."

"Will Cooper be at this ... deposition?"

"Yes, but he doesn't have to testify." Sensing the tension in my voice, he assured, "Don't worry. A court reporter, Duncan Norris, and I will also be present."

Butterflies fluttered in my stomach. "What exactly is Duncan looking for?"

"He's seeking information about your assets; particularly any investments you may have profited from during your marriage that Cooper would not have known about. Apparently, your ex thinks you have off-shore accounts. Duncan Norris will attempt to elicit testimony favorable to his client. In other words, to further inflate Cooper's bank account. He's after as much money as he can get from you. You will be sworn in, so you are required to answer all questions truthfully. If you have the slightest doubt about the meaning, don't answer. Ask for clarification."

"I'm afraid I'll say the wrong thing."

"We'll review questions that are normally asked." He paused, checking his appointments. "Is Thursday at 10:00 a.m. okay for a deposition preparation?" It was.

I hung up fuming. Cooper had initiated the divorce, and now he refused to sign the papers because he was a greedy jerk. I looked over the list of gifts that I had purchased for him. The more I thought about all I had spent on my selfish husband, the angrier I got. Deluding myself about him was a costly life lesson, emotionally and financially.

Watch	$8,600.00
Motorcycle	450.00
Electric bed	750.00
Luggage	500.00
New T.V.	500.00
Antique Gun	1000.00
Ring	4000.00
Miscellaneous Clothes	1000.00
Grand Total	$16,800.00

I remembered our weekly grocery trips and all the money I had spent on his choice succulent steaks. My only consolation was that the fat had settled on his waist.

The following Thursday, at the end of a hurried dry run, Harlan counseled, "Don't open a can of worms by volunteering additional information. Don't elaborate. During the inquiry, never forget that Cooper and Duncan are your adversaries." He smiled, "Be confident – you did well here. I know you'll do fine at the deposition."

As I gathered my purse and notebook, which by now was becoming extremely thick, he said, "I'll pick you up at 7:45 Friday morning."

"I'll be ready. Do you mind if my son and daughter join us? Not only for moral support but because I'm afraid of Cooper."

"He can't touch you. And your kids will have to remain in the reception area."

"My children can't stand him. They'd prefer not to be in the same room unless it's his funeral."

I knew Harlan was watching me as I walked toward the door. Did I still have the power to attract? I left the building walking a little taller!

On the day of the deposition, I dressed to impress in a red Liz Claiborne suit. Eat your heart out, Coop. Harlan rolled up in his shiny black BMW. Diane and Mark piled into the backseat. I sat next to Harlan, immersed in the aromas of Polo, the coffee he drank from a non-spill mug, and the rich leather interior of the car. He looked handsome in a tailored navy suit, azure button-down collar shirt, and matching power tie with sparkling diamond cufflinks. Harlan always dressed with meticulous care, as if he was going to a photo shoot for GQ magazine.

He asked Mark about current conditions in the stock market and which investments he favored, checking the health of his holdings. Mark's answers were impersonal and terse. He was still angry at me for marrying Cooper and putting my life in jeopardy. I was annoyed with my son. He could have been a little more pleasant. It hadn't been a cakewalk raising him (I dreaded parent/teacher conferences; he was not a studious kid). And dammit, I needed him now more than ever. People think that he burst forth onto Wall Street groomed, schooled, and ready. I was a fixture in the office at Central High School listening to complaints from teachers for assignments not turned in.

Diane was sunny and outgoing. My lack of appetite and Cooper's deceitfulness concerned her. "Mom, I'm worried he'll try to lure you back when he realizes he's not getting another dime."

"You don't have to worry; I'm not going back."

"Just be careful," she cautioned. "You're fragile."

We approached the Woodland exit, and Harlan smoothly guided the BMW off the interstate. The fall foliage was brilliantly singing hopefulness. The temperature hovered in the upper sixties. The trees were vivid shades of orange, red, yellow, and gold. I felt nostalgic, knowing this was my last trip to Woodland, my home for the four years.

Harlan drove to a three-story, red brick office building on Elm Street. In the 1800's this landmark was a bank. The large plate glass windows were beveled. Even the rough wood floors were original. A place of character, now used for the legal parting of characters.

There was no parking lot, so Harlan wedged his car in between a Ford truck and a beat-up Volkswagen on the street.

Diane spotted the "creep-mobile," Cooper's pickup, a block away.

"A five-pound bag of sugar in the gas tank wouldn't hurt," she said.

Mark sneered. "He deserves worse than that."

Harlan smiled, "Bad intentions are punishable by law."

"Killjoy," Diane mumbled.

I ignored their banter; my mind was on the gravity of the legal proceedings. I'd been praying since Harlan's call that I'd answer all the questions correctly. I was fed up with vandalism, extortion, interrogatories, and depositions. It was time to sign a paper and have our split finalized.

Harlan took my arm, "Remember, don't offer anything. Make Duncan ask."

The townspeople watched us with curiosity. We were as incongruous as any group that had entered this building. Harlan was the pricey legal eagle. I played the part of the carefree divorcée. Diane resembled Ashley Judd, and Mark, with the *Wall Street Journal* and *New York Times* tucked under his arm, was an unwilling tagalong. The sheriff and his soon to be ex would be the talk of the coffee shop. We marched up the steps to Duncan Norris' office. The secretary pointed to chairs for Diane and Mark before leading Harlan and me to an open door. Duncan rose from behind his desk and shook our hands. I was surprised at his dandified appearance – baby-faced handsome in a Leonardo DiCaprio kind of way.

My blood pressure shot up when I saw Cooper: in uniform, back to the wall, legs extended, his girth testing the small chair. He looked defeated before the proceedings had even begun. He was pathetic, not strong and invincible like the man who walked through my front door with his muscular arms full of firewood on our second date – the very night I fell in love. He reminded me of a big bully sitting outside the principal's office, waiting to receive a reprimand. I wasn't afraid. My lawyer and my children had my back.

Duncan Norris sat in a swivel chair behind his desk, the court reporter to his right. Harlan and I sat facing them. Cooper's eyes burned a hole through me. After covering boilerplate instructions and preliminary identity questions, Duncan got down to business. He was soft-spoken and compassionate, and at times his questions seemed no more than friendly conversation, typical attorney tactics to trick me into letting my guard down. At other times, the probes got excruciatingly personal and invasive. Whenever possible, I answered yes or no, knowing it did not completely answer the question.

For two hours, I fidgeted throughout the interrogation. Everyone's eyes were on me. Anyone who has never testified under oath as a deposition requires, cannot understand the trepidation a person feels. Would I be up to the task? Would my answers hurt my case and make Cooper rich? Then I thought, why should I worry – all I must do is tell the truth. Telling the truth requires no memorization; liars need great memories. I should have no concern over how the answer sounded or how I appeared.

Is the marriage irretrievably broken? Why? What are your assets? What are the accumulated debts? Who owns what? Who's entitled to what?

Cooper and I made no eye contact the entire two hours though he interrupted us with one comment I will never forget: "I love the woman. I always will."

For a long time, I clung to the lie that even though Cooper wanted my money, he was in love with me. I now realize that Cooper was not capable of loving anyone but himself. Dr. Phillips said he had an anti-social personality disorder with a distorted view of relationships. Cooper had a different kind of love that I didn't understand. He LOVED, loved me as long as he had something to gain. But when he stopped receiving, he started hating. He was simply buttering me up with his hand out.

When the interrogation was over, I hugged my children in the waiting area. Mark had finished reading his newspapers. Diane placed *Time* with a gun on the cover on top of the other magazines. Mark had mastered Wall Street – Diane had mastered the street. We trekked down the stairs. I was grateful to finish the deposition and let go of the stress. My children were relieved to be escorting me home in one piece.

As Harlan turned the key in the ignition, he said, "You handled the questions perfectly."

I felt I'd done a credible job and protected my nest egg. I mimicked Cooper's words, "I love the woman. I always will."

"Isn't that special," Diane said, impersonating Dana Carvey portraying Church Lady on *Saturday Night Live*. A wave of laughter filled the car.

I laughed along with my children, but my heart was heavy. We were making fun of a relationship that had once been precious to me.

As Harlan parked in my driveway, he asked me to gather some papers that he needed and send them to his office. We said goodbye. I unlocked the door and disarmed the security system, determined not to cry.

Twenty-nine

I smiled, appreciating the abundance of autumn color bursting from the trees as I rounded the corner leading to my home. Joggers passed me, parents played with their young children in the park, laughing and squealing with delight as their neon kites took flight in the breeze. Each day I walked the same route, just as I had on the lonely gravel roads at the farm. Except here in the city there were traffic, noise, pedestrians. Safety. I turned back to my home if I didn't see other people nearby. I had each curb, corner, and crack in the sidewalk ingrained in my memory. Unlocking the front door, I heard the phone jingle and hurried to the kitchen. "Mrs. Cowan," an unfamiliar voice said, "This is Jessica, the head paralegal at Weylan, Weylan, and Ridgebach. I don't know how to tell you this . . ."

"Tell me what?" I said concerned at the tone of her voice.

"We've misplaced your files."

"What do you mean you've misplaced my files? All of them?"

"Y-Yes," Jessica stammered, embarrassed that it was her responsibility to report this blunder.

My blood pressure began rising. "With your high-tech security, how could four huge folders disappear? I don't believe they walked out by themselves."

"I've instructed the staff to stop what they're doing and search."

"I handed you my entire financial history. Someone has my confidential information!"

"I'm so sorry," Jessica said as if it was all her fault. "This has never happened before."

"How can such a prestigious law firm lose vital paperwork? What if I said I lost my checkbook?"

She laughed nervously. "We're combing the office."

"I would hope so! I trusted Harlan to represent me, but he seems terribly distracted. Could my records be at his house?"

"He checked his car and home office. They weren't there."

I lost it. I wasn't sure I could summon the energy to plow through this latest aggravation. "I am appalled at your firm's lack of responsibility. I should charge the partners!"

The fact that I had made copies was of little comfort. Having already spent painstaking hours gathering my material from various file cabinets and desk drawers, I wasted the weekend standing in front of a copier, feeding one page at a time to reconstruct the lost data; examining every document, statement, receipt and 1099. Could my private information be buried in the city landfill or blowing down a street into a homeless person's hands to be carried into the bank? My name appeared on each page. Some of the forms had my Social Security number. When I delivered the folders to Jessica the second time, I should have attached a bill. I had paid a retainer. The firm's monthly statement came like clockwork. I suspect one of two scenarios: either Cooper bribed or slept with someone within the firm to steal my files, or Harlan's briefcase was taken by a random thief when he forgot to lock his car in his haste to enter a bar. No matter how much I wanted to blame it on Cooper, I believe it was the latter. Of many mishaps I encountered with my esteemed attorney, this one was the worst. So much for Jay Gold's recommendation.

Considering the exorbitant fees Harlan was charging, I wasn't getting a fair return on my money. According to rumor, Harlan was too preoccupied with women and booze to be bothered with the mundane task of preparing my case for court. Early in our association, he invited me to join him and friends for drinks. I was lonely and felt flattered to have the invitation. Harlan was to arrive at 7:00. At 7:30 I called time. I watched TV until 9:00, then slipped into my nightgown and hung up my clothes. I removed my makeup, watched the 10:00 news and went to bed. Now I'm relieved that our evening out never materialized. It was inappropriate for Harlan to invite a client to have a drink, and I had no business accepting. He was probably under the influence when he asked. My respect for Harlan deteriorated because of his lack of professionalism.

His voice was the loudest and his words the most compelling to stop me from yielding to Cooper's threat of extortion. Nevertheless, after Harlan's dramatic intervention and preparation for the deposition, our legal relationship became an exhausting game of mouse pursuing cat. No one could accuse me of pestering. I didn't call Harlan unnecessarily; and my questions were written and ready. He didn't show the same respect. His unavailability demanded that I open the lines of communication. I didn't expect daily updates, but I counted on him to return my calls promptly. I shouldn't have had to sit at my desk, pen in hand, writing several letters to his firm, explaining my needs and concerns. My patience was wearing thin from being in limbo. I wanted my marriage over so I could move on with my life.

I had two choices: change lawyers, or persuade Harlan to make my case a priority. A new firm would mean losing time and paying another retainer. I didn't want to dip further into my savings. Decisions were thrust upon me that I had never faced before. I began applying what my dad tried to teach me as a young girl. When exasperated with my indecisiveness, he would say, "It doesn't make any difference whether you are right or wrong. Just make a decision!"

The lesser of two evils was remaining with Harlan. To my surprise, taking the initiative felt right. I would gain more control of my divorce and have *my* needs met. I would no longer be a meek mouse, waiting for the cheese to come to me.

I came up with a plan to gain Harlan's attention and decided to go on an urban camping trip. My gear included a book, a sack lunch, and an attitude. Loretta dropped me off at the campsite – Harlan's office. "I'll call when I complete my mission," I said stepping out of her car, my chin up and shoulders back.

I marched in like I owned the place. Tiffany, Harlan's receptionist, looked at me quizzically and then at her appointment book. "Tell your boss I'm not leaving until I talk to him," I announced like I had every right to give the orders. Which I did. I was paying him.

She raised an eyebrow, perplexed at this breach of office etiquette. "Do you have an appointment?"

"I do now. Give Harlan my message, please."

"I'm sorry. It will have to wait. Mr. Ridgebach is in court all day."

"Then call court!"

There were no other clients waiting. I planted myself on the plush couch, my purse and provisions alongside. I snapped the ring on my can of Dr. Pepper for emphasis, opened my book, reached for my magnifier, and began reading. I finished a chapter and an apple. I could hear Tiffany murmuring on the telephone from her desk. An hour-and-a-half later, the phone rang. "Mrs. Cowan," she said, "please pick up the receiver on the table."

On the other end, Harlan sounded over-the-top. "Hi, Renee. How are you?"

I snarled something.

"I have great news," he said. "The judge has assigned a court date – December 15 at 10:00 a.m."

Smooth. Harlan knew how to deflect client anger! I wondered where he was calling from – possibly his couch at home or the golf course. I didn't care. Having attained a court date, I went home triumphant. My dormant feistiness had surfaced, and it was empowering.

The pre-divorce period became a dynamic lesson in assuming responsibility. I didn't have time to call Iris May or Rachel and opinion shop. I was learning to handle the day-to-day decisions myself. My wishbone had finally gotten out of the way of my backbone. This statement of independence was the most rewarding accomplishment of my life. I felt a surge of pride. Dad would be proud.

A real test of my assertiveness occurred in the corridor outside Harlan's office. We went toe-to-toe in an intense argument over a legal technicality. He stormed into his office and slammed the door so hard I visualized his class picture crashing to the floor, shards of jagged glass scattering. His reaction reminded me of Cooper stomping out the back door, kicking yard tools out of his way as he headed to the trees that bordered his farm when he was mad at me.

I turned to Jessica who was wide-eyed, watching the exchange from her cubicle adjacent to Harlan's office. "He's not used to female clients disagreeing with him," she whispered.

That I had the audacity to argue with him angered Harlan more than the issue involved.

I was beginning to recognize controlling, temperamental people, and I was tired of holding back my feelings to please everyone else. Harlan was a shorter, thinner, more refined version of Coop. It took time and the experience of contending with both men to begin to understand this destructive personality fully. Never again will I be controlled.

The long-awaited day, December 15, finally arrived. As I readied for Court, I felt calm and confident. Finally, it's going to be over. For many who experience divorce, it is a painful and reflective time. I was upbeat as I climbed into Harlan's Beemer for the drive to the same courthouse where Cooper and I had exchanged wedding vows three years earlier. I attributed my positive mood to knowing that I would now have Harlan and Cooper out of my life. As always when seeing him, I had made a conscious effort to look my best, and today I chose a new houndstooth suit. Let him be sorry for treating me like a castoff. I'm back on the market.

Harlan was in a congenial mood. Why wouldn't he be? The divorcée was paying a nice fat check for his services.

It had been a stressful week. Harlan and Duncan Norris had waited until the last minute to hammer out a financial agreement acceptable to both parties. Harlan had accomplished my priority – no more money for Cooper Cowan. He wouldn't get one more penny. I would love to have been the fly on the wall when Mr. Norris broke the news to him. Did he throw a tantrum with his attorney, or did he save his outbursts just for me? My accountant, Erica, had come to assist. As she left Harlan's office hours later, she lightened the mood, "Next time, have a prenuptial agreement drawn up."

I deserved that.

I laughed, "I'm not planning the next time. If there is, you can bet there will be more small print than on a credit card application."

Harlan and I chatted on our drive to the courthouse. The fighting was over. We had reached a truce. We arrived at the historic red brick building, built in 1904. A metal cupola adorned the top. The expanse of lawn and large trees occupied one square block.

Harlan pulled open the heavy door. We headed to the second floor for the hearing. Upon reaching the landing, I saw Coop in a flannel shirt and faded jeans, sprawled out on a wooden bench. We didn't speak. There was nothing more to say. Harlan and I waited near the door of the courtroom. At 9:45 we entered and sat at a table opposite the one occupied by Cooper and Duncan Norris. During our marriage, Cooper was the puppeteer and I the puppet with a painted-on smile. In the courtroom, we reversed roles. He was anxious and stressed – welcome to my world – as though he had lost his bankroll. He had. He was not Sheriff Cowan, cocky and in uniform. He was Mr. Cowan, morose and disheveled, while I was self-assured and for once, holding the upper hand. This little blonde was no longer his cash cow. He would have to go back to the cop shop and eat crow. No more big talk.

Cooper could no longer scare me. I had lived with his temper; his rage; his words of contempt; his manipulations and threats. I had heard of his power over others, his scare tactics, and strong arming. I had seen firsthand the property damage and felt his bodily harm. I had lived through the worst of it and come out on top.

"All rise," The bailiff bellowed. "Court is now in session with The Honorable Judge Crane presiding." With a flourish of his black robe, the judge took his seat at the bench. The proceedings were routine. Before ruling, the judge asked, "Do you want to retain your married name?" My mind raced. Confusion. Indecision. For months, I had struggled with this internal debate. Cooper's actions had stripped me of my self-confidence, wreaked havoc in familial relationships, threatened physical harm and financial ruin. The name was our last tie. Did I want to drop Cowan, which I had committed to for the rest of my life?

I replied, "No. I'd like to take back my maiden name." The right decision.

The judge said, "The court hereby finds that the divorce decree should be granted and the court so rules." With a bang of the gavel, my marriage ended. Harlan put his hand on my shoulder, "You did an excellent job." He gathered his papers. Duncan shook Harlan's hand and exchanged a few pleasantries. We passed Coop on our way out. He had moved to a long bench at the rear of the courtroom to wait for Mr. Norris. His only words were, "Duchess misses you." He said this to the back of my head as we passed.

I never saw Cooper or Duchess again. I should have asked if I could keep her. Later his mother told me he had accidentally backed over her in his driveway. She died from her injuries. I was sick. It was no accident. He knew how much Duchess and I loved one another.

Harlan took my arm as we descended the steps to drive back to the city. We stopped at a countryside café to toast the outcome with coffee. As I climbed the steep step into the restaurant, his hand cupped the small of my back, securing the continuation of our lawyer/client relationship.

As we made small talk, I was still floating on a high, knowing my battles with Cooper were finally over.

"We nailed him," Harlan said.

Yes, *we* did.

He encouraged me to call with questions about future legal matters; I could hear the cash register in his head going cha-ching. He dismissed my correspondence to him, the unreturned phone calls, hours of wrangling and his temper tantrums. I wanted to forget anything related to legalities. He paid the bill, and we climbed into his car for the ride to my house.

As I watched Harlan's BMW roll down my driveway, my euphoria faded. For years Cooper had controlled my life – how I would fill my days to suit him and then how to get rid of him without endangering my life. Indisputably, I had walked in my husbands' shadow. After December 15, the pages of my daily planner were blank. I no longer had anything on my schedule. I called friends to tell them that I was a free woman.

Sara, my friend and life coach, cautioned. "You will always have to look over your shoulder."

At the time, I didn't grasp the meaning of her words. All I felt was a profound sense of emptiness. It would be years before I fully comprehended how close I had come to being destroyed.

Since that time, I have learned that in spite of his drinking and womanizing, Harlan didn't drop the ball when it came to my divorce. The fact that I walked away from my marriage without Cooper getting more of my money is a testament to Harlan's capabilities. Jay was right – Harlan didn't back down.

Thirty

Two weeks following my acrimonious divorce, Diane bounced into the kitchen, giving me a bear hug. She brought lunch – takeout from the neighborhood Chinese restaurant. A few hours alone with my daughter and savory oriental cuisine. What could be better?

I had spent the last fourteen days trying to recover from the damage done by my ex. My marriage was over on paper, but not yet internally. There were times I still missed him; wondered if divorce was the right thing. Although knowing what I know now, I'd never want him back. I was exhausted from the last year's shenanigans. It felt good to have a reason to smile.

"Hope you're hungry," Diane said cheerfully, setting small, square white containers filled with Broccoli Chicken, Mongolian Beef, egg rolls and fortune cookies on the counter as if we were sumo wrestlers in training.

"How many people are you expecting to join us?" I laughed, laying out placemats, silverware, and napkins. No chopsticks. Niki warmed up a spot under the table waiting for dropping morsels.

The ring of the telephone broke the festive mood. "Good timing," I sighed, going to the desk to pick up.

"How are you?" Margo asked in her smoker's voice.

My shoulders tensed. The last time I talked to Margo, she delivered Cooper's fifty grand demand, and I wasn't sure how to answer. Before I got a chance, she said, "There's something I haven't told you."

I waited. Silent.

"Cooper had several affairs while you were married. Was I wrong not to tell you?"

My spine stiffened. My throat tightened as I tried to absorb this brazen admission of deceit on Margo's part as well as Cooper's. In my head I screamed, "You were my best friend! Yes, you should have told me!" The room pitched. I sat down heavily. As her cutting words sank in, I watched Diane unwrap an eggroll, pinch off a corner, and pass the treat under the table to Niki – just like she did with her mini poodle Sophie, when she was a little girl and thought no one was looking.

Stunned, I said, "I wouldn't have believed you."

Women that Cooper and I had known flashed before my eyes. Was it Mona? Irene? The red-headed waitress at Jenny's who had a crush on him? She did always call him "hun." Or Margo? And when did this start? Now I wish I had asked who he had slept with, (so I could hate them, also) but I was too shocked to collect my thoughts.

"There's one more thing," Margo said.

"What the hell, now?"

"A year ago, I was weeding my flower bed when Cooper pulled up in his cruiser. He sat down on a step and asked, 'Did you know Renee has a boyfriend?'"

"I was astounded. 'She's not that kind of woman. Besides she's so in love with you.'"

"'Since you're her best friend, I thought you'd know. Well, got to get back to work.' He jumped in his cruiser and was gone."

"Sure, Margo. Did I hop on my seeing-eye horse and gallop off to a rendezvous? He would have killed me! Unlike him, I was faithful! I'm having lunch. I've got to go." I hung up and turned to Diane, "Damn Cooper! He cheated on me!"

She hesitated for a minute, then said, "And that surprises you? I suspected it from the day I met him. Remember, the two of you came to the hospital when Jon was born? Cooper's eyes lingered on me too long. The hair on the back of my neck stood up. He looked the cute nurse up and down. I knew that he was a pig!"

"Why didn't you tell me?"

"I was afraid that if I said anything, you would defend him and be mad at me."

"You're probably right. I was constantly making excuses for Cooper. From the beginning of our relationship, he swore that he would always be faithful."

Diane said, "I remember him bragging one evening at dinner, 'You can be anybody you want when you're fifty miles from home.'"

"So that's how he carried on his affairs – driving to the next county. How could I not know?"

The truth is I didn't want to know.

"Why did Margo wait until now to tell you? Where was she when he was screwing around?" Diane snapped.

"She couldn't tell me at the time because I would have confronted Cooper. He'd know where I got my information and ruin her 'spotless' reputation.' At least I don't live in Woodland anymore. I don't have to wonder if every woman I see in town might be one of his playmates."

Cooper had no respect for our marital vows. He was a hypocrite, always declaring that he would never beat me or be unfaithful. Both proved to be a lie.

Thirty-one

What had possessed me to move in with and marry a man who criticized me relentlessly, no matter how hard I tried to please him? *"That maroon blouse makes you look old. My mother thinks you're robbing the cradle."*

Why didn't I defend myself when he used my vision as a weapon to hurt me? *"I told you your eyesight is getting worse. You looked right through me when you and Janet drove through town today."*

Not to mention leaving my spacious, three bedrooms, four and one-half bath home in the city for Cooper's dusty, mice infested, isolated farmhouse with only one bathroom that we had to share.

Initially, our relationship was ideal. We spent two weeks in flirtatious phone conversations, followed by three dates on which Cooper treated me like royalty. On our fourth date, the bubble burst. Cooper began finding fault with me. From that day forward, our relationship was bipolar, either the highest of highs or the lowest of lows. I never knew which Cooper would surface. Knowing the highs would not last, I lived in fear, waiting for him to explode.

Cooper was astute, identifying my weaknesses to use to his advantage. Naïveté, loneliness, and low self-esteem were easy targets for him to exploit. Once he identified my vulnerabilities, he knew how to control me. I feel certain that he did a background check, discovering that I had money in the bank – exactly what he was searching to find. To avoid becoming involved in another Dr. Jekyll/Mr. Hyde relationship, I had to understand what was in my DNA that led me to fall in love with a con man. The search would take me back to my childhood.

I'm 11 years old, frowning at my reflection in the bathroom mirror: horn-rimmed glasses, pigtails, one big ear. I can hear Aunt Sybil's bossy voice call from my bedroom, "Don't wear black jeans and a yellow blouse together! You look like a bumble bee. Cousin Bonnie would never dress like that." I was sick and tired of hearing her name. It was always Bonnie this, Bonnie that! Nevertheless, knowing Aunt Sybil would not let up, I changed my clothes.

Aunt Sybil, Mom's older sister, frequently visited us in Omaha. Probably not as often as I recall, but her overbearing presence made it seem as if she had moved in. For me, it was punishment, not a friendly visit. Instead of staying in the guest bedroom at the end of the hallway, she chose to invade my privacy and slept on the other twin bed in my room, with only a tiny nightstand between us. I had to learn to sleep with the lights and radio on because she was either reading or listening to Amos and Andy and Milton Berle over the airwaves.

I moved around the house silently and discreetly, never wanting to call attention to myself. I remember a time repeating a story my friends had told me. My Aunt said, "Don't be ridiculous. You don't know what you're talking about." Another day while making my bed, she walked in and snapped, "You're doing it wrong." She made me feel small and stupid.

When my sisters, Joany and Carol, and I were young, our parents took us on annual vacations to visit Mom's family in Oklahoma City. Hot and tired from the ten-hour drive, we descended on Aunt Sybil and Uncle Jim at the Shawnee Tower, a spacious apartment hotel in the heart of downtown. Aunt Sybil, the image of beautiful actress Ida Lupino, greeted us with affection, showering my sisters and me with hugs and bright red lipstick kisses. Her breath smelled of stale Maxwell House coffee and Pall Mall cigarettes. Their furnished apartment lacked warmth and contained only a few personal items. It may as well have been a room at the Howard Johnson's down I-35. The focal point was my grandmother's mahogany roll-top desk with various drawers and pigeon holes, where Aunt Sybil attended to correspondence and bill paying. Next to a green blotter trimmed in gold, sat a 5x7 framed photo of my aunt, manager of costume jewelry at Rosenbaum's, headquarters of the family-owned jewelry chain. In the photo, her glasses rested on the tip of her nose as she showed a sparkling bangle bracelet to a customer. A cherished black and white portrait of the Shoshone's – my mother's family – with five of their six children decked out in their best clothes, hung on the wall. It was taken shortly after their seasick voyage from Russia. The youngest child, Aunt Klara, was born in Kansas City, Missouri. My grandfather's last name in his hometown of Gomel was Schrchan but was changed to Shoshone upon entry to America, perhaps because of the language barrier. Grandmother's daughters inherited her beauty and her need to dominate; their sons acquired Grandfather's playful sense of humor. Mother was a spunky eighteen-month-old in the photograph.

During our Oklahoma City visits, my father always accompanied Uncle Jim to his executive job at Rosenbaum's. Uncle Jim was responsible for introducing the fine jewelry, marketing, and merchandising. Dad liked observing the operations of the fourteen stores located in Oklahoma and Texas. His suggestions carried great weight and the family incorporated many of them. I am proud that my father had the drive to start his own business, Micklin Lumber Company, in Omaha, Nebraska. He employed most of his extended family, giving them an opportunity in the new country.

The morning after our arrival, Mom and Aunt Sybil, still in cotton housecoats, settled at the kitchen table. I joined them, anticipating juicy gossip. A fresh pot of coffee sat on a trivet by the ashtray. A pack of cigarettes lay alongside their cups. Comparing the eight nieces was a frequent topic of conversation, which I dreaded. Each of us had been labeled with self-fulfilling prophecies. Stephanie was considered the prettiest and sweetest; Bonnie, always good with a quick come-back and the ability to mix and match outfits; Lavonne, the most popular; Jean the quietest and most perceptive, and Sherry, the baby we all loved to spoil. Joany, Carol, and I held the dubious honor of being characterized as the smartest. I was too young to appreciate that intelligence might be more important to my future than looks and popularity.

Aunt Sybil eyed me, taking measure since our last visit. Her mouth was set firm; eyes hard and intense. I braced myself. What she saw was a kid in glasses, lacking self-esteem; in other words, an easy target.

As I savored rye toast smothered in butter, she chided, "You look ridiculous, sitting there like Raggedy Ann with your hair falling in your face. Do you ever comb it?" I flinched as she pushed my bangs off my forehead.

I bit my lip and made a lame attempt to defend myself. "All my friends wear their hair this way."

"I wouldn't take you to a dogfight, let alone shopping. Why do I waste my breath? You still don't know how to put on a belt. Don't ever embarrass me again in front of a saleswoman."

I looked at Mom. Why didn't she defend me? I was hurt and confused when she said, "Listen to your aunt, she knows fashion." I internalized the sisters' criticism because I was afraid to stand up to them.

Aunt Sybil lit a cigarette with her silver monogrammed lighter. I fantasized her heavily lacquered beehive going up in flames and giggled to myself. Why didn't I join my sisters playing in the next room? Instead, I sat in fascinated horror. Like a child watching a scary movie through spread fingers, I sat transfixed.

I fought the back tears but was afraid to defy her. I complained to Mom later in private, "Why does Aunt Sybil hate me? She's constantly putting me down."

"She doesn't hate you; she loves you. That's why she takes the time and trouble to help you."

Why didn't I rebel? No one encouraged me to be assertive. Instead, they trained me to "shut up and listen."

There was another reason I tolerated Aunt Sybil's abuse. I didn't want to miss the highlight of these vacations – our awesome shopping trips. I relinquished my self-respect for a wardrobe.

Since our family used the barter system, we got our clothes wholesale. Two exclusive merchants, Mr. Greenspan of the Avenue, and Mr. Moss of Barton-Moss rolled out the proverbial red carpet. In turn, Mrs. Greenspan had a passion for rubies, and Mrs. Moss loved diamonds, which they purchased at cost from Rosenbaum's.

On these visits, my workaholic aunt took time off from her job to make sure that I looked ready for the runway. I had reached the magical manic teens, which was Mom's gauge for when young women should start paying attention to the styles that graced the pages of Seventeen magazine. She set the bar high – maybe a little too high. My wardrobe was considered essential preparation for womanhood. I had to polish my image for the world to see. How you looked was more important than how you felt.

At 9:45 a.m. sharp, Mom, Aunt Sybil, my sisters, and I, dressed to the nines, emerged from the elevator and trekked six blocks to The Avenue. Although it wasn't yet noon, the temperature soared to ninety-one degrees. Trying on the latest styles was the only reason I'd want to leave the cool comfort of the apartment and be in my Aunt's hateful company. Mr. Greenspan hurried to receive hugs from Mom and Aunt Sybil, acknowledging my sisters and me with dreaded cheek-pinching and the customary comment, "You girls have grown so much taller since last year." He summoned a saleswoman who knew how to ingratiate. Trendy, fall fashions decorated the racks, which Mom and my aunt were more than happy to inspect, then make selections. The shopping junkets with Aunt Sybil and Mom were a teenage girl's dream. We walked out loaded down with boxes in flowery wrapping. The finery seemed worth my aunt's toxic words. We left our purchases behind the credit counter at Rosenbaum's and headed to Barton-Moss to go merch mad again.

Although Aunt Sybil was often ruthless and judgmental, she could hide it behind a plastic smile. The day we arrived, and the day we left, she enfolded me in the pretense of love. Even at a young age, I wondered why she faked kindness. Since I had internalized criticism to signify love, I kept returning for more. My junior year in college I transferred from the University of Nebraska to the University of Oklahoma and saw my aunt frequently. She was a Shoshone through and through and remained dominating, quick to criticize and always knew what was best for me. Uncle Jim was the only family member to empathize. He pulled me aside one day after she had chastised me for a comment I'd made, and said, "Your aunt should not treat you that way." Though he never mentioned her bullying again, it helped to know I had a secret ally. The rest of the family seemed to ignore Aunt Sybil's persecution of me. Perhaps they were relieved not to be on the receiving end of her forked tongue. Why was I Aunt Sybil's scapegoat?

And why did Mom allow her sister to continually attack me? It took me years to put it together. The sisters never found fault with one another. If Aunt Sybil had ever claimed that the sky was red, my mother never would have corrected, saying, "No, it's blue." They were always in total agreement.

Mom and Aunt Sybil, as well as Aunt Klara, were strong, outspoken women. You were not to challenge their viewpoints. You couldn't fight a system like that. The Shoshone sisters were thick as thieves. There were many times I hoped my Dad would intercede on my behalf. It never happened. He idolized my mother, and I never heard him find fault with her. His world revolved around her. It was an emotionally laden situation. I wish, like Uncle Jim, Dad had said, "This is wrong. Your aunt has no right to talk to you that way."

In business, Dad was a force to be reckoned with; at home, Mother was the force. My parents worried about the long-term effects of my eye disease and didn't understand that the emotional abuse I suffered would have far more devastating repercussions. As a result, they sacrificed my emotional well-being.

Following Boots' death, Aunt Sybil stayed at my house. Her kind face briefly surfaced. Haunted by the image of my husband's body, it terrified me that the impression would forever terrorize my nights. She comforted, "That's what you said when your dad died. Time helps erase the starkness of death." Aunt Sybil's consoling words eased my fear. Three days after laying Boots to rest, she warned, "If you don't get a handle on these unruly children, you'll never find another husband."

At a time when I needed support more than ever, she attacked my parenting skills. I'd just buried Boots and couldn't handle her malicious comments. I drove to a friend's house two blocks away and called my cousin, Stephanie, who had returned to Denver following the funeral.

"How can I get Aunt Sybil out of my house? I can't take one more of her derogatory remarks." Stephanie sympathized and made me promise to go back to my home and stand up for myself. I didn't keep my promise. I drove home feeling deflated. In Aunt Sybil's eyes, I never did anything right. Not seeing that criticism was not acceptable as much as everyone else, it's easy to let others be right every time. She finally left two weeks later.

After revisiting my past, I understand how it impacted my life and why I felt devalued. Dr. Philipps once told me, "We tend to go with what we know." Having grown up with criticism that supposedly expressed love, it wasn't surprising to repeat it in marriage. Cooper was a greed-driven version of Aunt Sybil in size fourteen cowboy boots.

Thirty-Two

One Sunday morning, when Cooper and I were spending a weekend in the city, we sipped coffee while waiting for breakfast at the Pancake House. My neighbor Becky, and her husband Neal entered through the swinging doors, and I asked them to join us. I hadn't seen her in years.

Becky is a 5' 1", pixie-like dynamo. She is non-judgmental and endowed with a wealth of positive qualities: confident, focusing her attention on you, never speaking ill of anyone. She has styled her coal black hair in a Dorothy Hamill wedge; oversized costume jewelry, large hoop earrings, bangle bracelets, and Bohemian style clothing; long flowery skirts and soft blouses are her signature look.

We met when Gail and Mark were in grade school through Trouping Theater, a charitable organization that put on plays at child care centers and the Omaha Playhouse for Children with Special Needs. She was the director, and I couldn't sing or dance, so I played the part of a rooster. Yes, feathers, clucking, cock-a-doodle-doo, the whole works. I strutted around the stage in costume with the other characters. The children's giggles and squeals and applause at the end made it an entertainment success.

There are few people with whom I would share my ambitions for fear they would devalue or ridicule them. I knew that I could trust Becky. After steaming plates of food were served, I surprised myself by blurting, "A longtime dream of mine is to host a talk show."

I snuck a look at my husband to see his reaction. He stared at me curiously, chewing his bacon, but said nothing, which was shocking. If he had forbidden it, I would have abandoned the idea. His face remained indifferent.

"What's stopping you?" Becky asked, waving to a patron who had just walked in the door but never taking her eyes off me.

"It seems like a pipe dream."

"You never know until you try. Give me a call when you're ready to begin. I have contacts with the local media. I'll help you."

After Cooper and I had divorced, I reconsidered my priorities. I would no longer depend on a man to provide me with an identity. I had been down that road too many times. I began to set career goals.

A job would give purpose and structure to my life; an aspect that had always been missing. However, I didn't have a work background except as a young woman in sales. Retail, looking back, was a very gratifying position. Maybe nostalgia made the memory rosier than the experience, such as sore feet and the occasional cantankerous customer, now not even acknowledged in my newfound lust for joining the nine-to-five workforce. My philosophy was like my blood type, B positive.

I called Becky.

"How have you been?" she asked, glad to hear from me.

"I recently moved back to the city. Cooper and I are divorced."

"I'm sorry to hear that."

"Don't be. Do you recall our conversation about my dream to host a talk show?"

"Of course. Are you ready?"

"Will you still help me?"

"Absolutely," she said with her customary zeal. "Why don't you come for coffee and we'll map out a strategy? I don't work Wednesdays."

I have long admired Becky's entrepreneurial gutsiness. She owns a successful advertising agency. Like Barbara Mandrel sings: "I was country when country wasn't cool," Becky was active in business at a time when only a few women had broken through the glass ceiling. She has always encouraged us to pursue our dreams, whether clerical, entrepreneurial, creative or soccer mom.

At the appointed hour, I walked two short blocks to Becky's house, excited at the prospect of expanding my horizons. It was a golden October day, with sunshine burnishing the mums and cool air spinning brilliant leaves onto the yards. I rang the bell at the modern brick ranch. She welcomed me with a dishtowel over her shoulder. I followed her to the kitchen, listening carefully to avoid tripping over her dog. We sat at her pedestal table. She filled our cups with fragrant coffee.

"Did you jot down some ideas?" she asked.

"I need help. Where do I start?"

I sipped coffee, watching her over my cup. If posies can grow through cracks in concrete, I could succeed with Becky's guidance.

"Write down topics for ten shows," she began. "Include a list of guests. Paint a clear picture of the time frame for each interview. When you finish the proposal, I'll take it to the program director at Channel 1 for evaluation and, I hope, approval." Becky was going out on a limb to help my dream become a reality.

Caught up in her enthusiasm, I had an imaginary Rolodex of potential guests in mind by the time I returned home. I called Diane to share the possibility of an exhilarating career opportunity and asked my creative daughter to help write the proposal.

"Let's start Sunday," she said, knowing my inclination to procrastinate.

The new me, though, had no intention of backing out. I needed to prove something to myself; that I could be more than a wife. If I quit this, I'd be abandoning myself.

On a clear, cold morning, with a Big Chief tablet, my souvenir cop cup (thanks to Cooper. That's about all I got.) full of pens, and a pot of hot coffee, we were ready to create my vision of a ground-breaking talk show. Putting our pens to paper, we brainstormed, debated, and filled the wastebasket with wadded sheets until we agreed on the most thought-provoking topics and guests: local successful business owners, women entering the workforce after being stay-at-home mothers or taking a position that only men had occupied previously, exercise, nutrition, and fashion.

I delivered the 10-page proposal to Becky and waited for the phone to ring. Three weeks later my mentor called with the disappointing news. "The director said, 'Not at this time.' He likes the idea, but there isn't a slot between the national and local lineup. He's going to keep your proposal in mind in case he gets an opening. I'm really sorry."

My new mantra was "Never give up." I had a backup plan. A week later, Becky and I took our dogs for a walk, and I shared Plan B. "I'm thinking of another way to turn my gift of gab into a profession. During my second marriage, I spoke pro bono on various topics."

"Where, and on what?" Becky asked surprised to learn this about my past.

"Locally, to groups on widowhood."

We stopped as the dogs sniffed a fire hydrant, right around the corner from my near miss with death.

"Is there a subject you're passionate about?"

"I've decided on women and finance. I'm savvy about savings and investing. Having been widowed and divorced, I know how important it is for women to take charge of and manage their money."

"It's essential to be well prepared," Becky said. "Become an authority."

Becky's mind was on fast forward, "You must serve an apprenticeship. What about obtaining a list of non-profit organizations from the Chamber of Commerce? Write a letter explaining you're an experienced speaker and give a brief bio. List any subjects you feel qualified to speak on. Include references. And remember, the work you choose now may not be what you'll pursue in a year."

Nebraska Small Business Development helped me find contacts, and Becky's agency designed a classy brochure. She arranged for me to have an interview on a local radio show. When the program ended, I was depressed. It had fallen short of my expectations. I ended up on Diane's front porch, whining that it had been a waste of time.

"What did you expect to happen?"

"The host didn't mention my speaking goals. It was weird. He focused on widowhood. That happened so long ago."

I was discouraged, but instead of dwelling on what I thought was a failure, my usual habit, I dove into my business books, determined to increase my knowledge of economics. I would prove that I knew my subject backward and forward and could answer questions under pressure.

I spoke to a career advisor who urged me to join Toastmasters International to improve my speaking skills. Self-conscious about my eyesight and afraid the members wouldn't like me, I had to push myself to attend the first meeting. After joining, I postponed making my first speech until I ran out of excuses. When I finally gathered the courage, the group was very supportive. Along with pointing out our weak areas, members and leaders always praised us for our strengths. Throughout the years I was an active member, I never left a meeting feeling stupid.

All my life I was accustomed to destructive criticism. Toastmasters offered constructive suggestions. That's when I learned it's all in the delivery. The club validated my speaking progress and personal worth, and three years later voted me Division Governor of the Year and presented me with a plaque. Much to my surprise, I discovered I had natural leadership abilities and made friends easily. It was a life-changing experience at a critical time.

I continued speaking, at no cost, at luncheons and churches to build my skills. Gradually I began charging a small fee. I soon realized that, though trying hard, I would never make it as a professional speaker. I was always nervous. My delivery sounded robotic like the programmed voice from your cell phone.

Then a wonderful opportunity came my way. The University of Nebraska at Omaha hired me to conduct a workshop on the language barrier between men and women: you know, the *Men are from Mars, Women are from Venus* phenomenon. A workshop, as opposed to a speech, is where everyone participates. I had guidelines to follow, but it was pretty much open discussion. Unlike a class, I wasn't a teacher. Interacting with the participants felt natural and was stimulating. I decided to apply to other colleges to see if they could use my expertise. A director at Metropolitan Community College hired me to lead a series of workshops for singles. Some of the topics I chose were: self-esteem, finance, dating, and friendships.

Before my first class, Diane helped me with my hair and makeup. I took inventory of my briefcase: huge note cards with oversized writing in front, notebook behind them, extra paper in the back, Sharpie pens in the front zipper pocket, and breath mints. I gave her a hug as she wished me luck.

When my driver and I arrived at the Education Center, a young man at the front desk directed us to my assigned classroom. As I arranged my material on the podium, twenty-five men and women of varying ages trickled in and settled on chairs in a semi-circle. Surprisingly I felt comfortable.

I introduced myself. "Welcome to *Playing Singles in a Doubles Game.* I am looking forward to our getting to know one another. I'll begin by telling you a few things about myself. I have three adult children. I was widowed when they were young, remarried and divorced twice. My last husband was abusive, but that's a whole other class. We can discuss it in the future if you like. I would never want to repeat those years, but it put me in the real world, and since then I no longer take people at face value. I have always wanted to achieve more than being a wife and mother. That might be for some of you, and that's fine. But I felt something was missing. That's why I'm here on the other side of this lectern."

The session was running smoothly. Many were taking part in the discussion, trusting the group with their hopes and fears. I didn't so much teach as participate in the healing dynamic. I thrived on their energy and enthusiasm. I had not only found a reason to get up each morning, but I loved what I was doing. The students evaluated me after each workshop. My scores were reassuringly high.

My position lasted six years. One day the director phoned, "Your workshops have been excellent, but I want to take a new direction." I thanked him. I too was ready for another challenge.

Work was now my priority, but not for a paycheck or benefits. Another man wasn't important. I hadn't completely broken the habit, and still window-shopped. Why not? But the temptation to invest was tempered by caution. If anyone knows that relationships don't last forever, it's me. One husband died, the second walked away, and number three was a con man.

Thirty-three

I awoke in a panic and glanced at the clock – 1:00 a.m., I'd only slept forty-five minutes. I fought free of the clammy sheets. Perspiration was dripping off me; my hair felt drenched, nightgown sticking to my trembling body; I questioned God, "What is happening to me?" My eyes were red and swollen from lack of sleep. My cheeks were hollow, and clothing that had once complimented my physical attributes now hung on me. Is this a nervous breakdown? If so, why?

Some of the symptoms I was now experiencing appeared to have aspects of repressed mourning, confusing me. I thought I'd worked through the pain of divorcing Cooper. Tears over him had dried up long ago. A grief manual had been my roadmap to survival. I had faced the multitude of feelings: sadness, anger, bargaining, *I should have bought the land*. Indelibly etched in my mind were the repercussions of delayed mourning. An incident in a psychology seminar triggered memories of my father's death, years earlier.

The phone rang in the small apartment that Boots and I rented the first two years of our marriage. I looked at the kitchen clock – 10:00 a.m. It was Cleo, our loyal housekeeper. She had been with the family for nine years. A tall black woman, she had strong facial features, was gracious, trustworthy, and devoted to us. Since Mom was in Oklahoma City attending Stephanie's wedding, I assumed my sixteen-year-old sister Carol, brown curly hair, big brown eyes, too cute for her own good, was late for school and needed a ride. Cleo sounded worried, "I've been pounding on your dad's door. Breakfast is ready, but he doesn't answer."

My father was on bed rest nursing a heart condition.

"I'm on my way," I said.

I grabbed my car keys and purse and headed for my parents' home, a mile away. Cleo met me at the back door. I hurried through the kitchen to the marble entry way and up the spiral staircase of the elegant brick house that Dad had built when my sisters and I were young. Cleo was right behind me. I pushed open the bedroom door. "Dad!" I cried, rushing to his side. He was slumped over in bed, in his pajamas. Though sunlight streamed through the windows, his bedside lamp was on. A favorite book, The Prophet, by Kahlil Gibran, had slid half off his lap. I kept pleading, "Dad, please wake up." I shook his shoulder. No response. Cleo finally pulled me away.

When she heard the news, Mom was devastated and booked the next flight home. Boots and my father-in-law rushed in the back door. Dave tried to give me a hug. I turned away. I didn't want someone else's father consoling me. I wanted my dad back. Joany returned immediately from her freshman year at Sarah Lawrence College in New York.

Boots and I drove to Central High School to pick up Carol. How was I going to tell her Dad was dead?

Years later Carol dropped a bomb on me. "The night Dad died I was on a date. I came home at 10:30 and stopped in his room to kiss him goodnight. At first, I thought he was sleeping. Then I knew he wasn't. I went to bed. The next morning, I left for school."

Afraid to let her secret out, she had carried the guilt all these years.

Why didn't she call 911? If the paramedics had arrived, it's possible they could have saved him. She never said.

Dad was a voracious reader and passed that joy on to us. One of my cherished memories occurred when I was nine years old. He and I were driving downtown and drove by the library. He pointed at the gold brick building, bordered with intricate medallions under the cornice and said, "Everything you need to know is in there."

I didn't realize until early adulthood how much I cherished him. His pale, frail presence at my wedding was a painful reminder of heart disease caused by rheumatic fever in his teens, which resulted in his early death. He had aged years beyond fifty-one. At the end of the ceremony, he stood by himself, softly crying. His daughter was going forward to a new life. The only other time I remember his tears was when his father died.

My anguish was fresh as though it had happened yesterday; a deep sorrow came over me for days. No matter how long it had since my father died, I still missed him. When my husband Boots died, I was thirty-seven and experienced shock, numbness, fear, guilt, but in time came to terms with my loss.

While married to Donald, I interviewed Lee Anne for my first book. Her husband was killed in Vietnam. Her family had lived by the tenet: keep a stiff upper lip. She had bottled up her grief while going through the motions of daily life. Eventually, she remarried. A year later, LeeAnne and her husband were at a church retreat when something in the minister's sermon sparked memories of her deceased spouse. She started sobbing uncontrollably, finally going through the depression stage. Perhaps Lee Anne thought that she and Anthony hadn't had enough time together, then after he was gone, she had a hard time helping the kids deal with their grief. She had spent too long in the denial stage. LeeAnne said it was far more painful than if she'd grieved immediately. It's like cutting your foot. If you fail to treat the wound, infection sets in that will prolong convalescence.

The next morning, I was anxious that I might suffer a panic attack while presiding over the Toastmasters meeting that evening. I had recently been named the president of my chapter. I was afraid that I would never be able to drag myself out the door, but I knew that I would feel worse if I locked myself inside my home and neglected my responsibility. I applied makeup and put on a sharp outfit, hoping I wouldn't sweat through my blouse or hyperventilate during the meeting. Although shaky, I managed to get through my required time at the head of the group. When it ended, I still felt like my knees would buckle.

Trish, a fellow Toastmaster, drove me home. Feeling desperate and sensing that she could be trusted, I confided, "I don't know what's the matter with me. I'm falling apart. I can't continue the pretense."

She looked at me puzzled. "You always seem so confident. We thought you had it all together."

I looked out the window at the passing street lights. "It shows how little we can tell about people from outward appearances." I had been successful in creating the façade that I wanted to be the truth. I was living up to the standards set by my mother.

"You're not thinking of hurting yourself, are you?"

"No. I'm frightened but would not take my life."

The following day Dr. Phillips had an opening, and I made an appointment. He was my last hope. He greeted me with his usual warmth and reserve. I settled on the small couch in his quiet office. I was afraid to admit how panicky I felt, as if uttering the words would make my self-diagnosis correct; that I was having a nervous breakdown and would end up sedated in the loony bin with other mental cases. We sat there awhile like the taxi driver waiting for instructions and the passenger unsure of her destination. Nevertheless, the therapy meter was running. I glanced at my notes, written so large that a few words filled a page. The letters blurred together. The enormity of my situation hit me like a semi, and the floodgates opened. I buried my face in my hands. Dr. Phillips handed me a box of Kleenex and put the trash can within my reach.

"What's wrong with me? I feel like I've fallen into a well and can't climb out. I can't sleep. I feel jittery. I have no appetite. My daughter is trying to force feed me Fritos to help me gain back some weight."

Without hesitation, he said, "You are learning to be alone for the first time in your life."

I shook my head stubbornly, like a kid refusing his bitter medicine. "I've never worried about solitude. As a child, I had several good friends but enjoyed playing by myself for hours."

I value my time alone. It's wired in me. The many hours I spent in my room as a young girl sheltered me. Within those beige walls, my life was manageable in my safe place.

"Your parents were in the wings. Your sisters were nearby."

Joany and Carol were four and six years younger and had different interests and friends. I had a vivid imagination and loved being outside near our magnificent rose garden, which bloomed from May to the first frost. Blossoms in sunset hues of dark red, yellow, orange, and pink graced our side yard beneath the living room windows. During summer vacation, I would sit on a blanket in the backyard under a large shade tree with my nose buried in a book. Some of my favorites were *The Little Colonel Series, Nancy Drew Mysteries, The Secret Garden,* and *A Girl of the Limberlost.* When I wasn't devouring these pages, I played with paper dolls. I cut clothing and accessories from department store catalogs and designed their wardrobes. I spent hours acting out daily life with my paper dolls. They went shopping, to the movies, and dressed fancy for dates. Looking back, it was an outlet for me; a way to express myself, which was rarely accepted by my family. When I walked in a room, it seemed my elders were always judging me.

The ice tinkling in Dr. Phillips glass as he took a sip of water brought me back to the present. I looked at him doubtfully. "I was a widow."

"You had children to raise. They kept you going."

"When Donald and I divorced, the older kids were away at college," I argued.

"You began looking for a new partner. One of the important things to learn in life is how to be with yourself, and some people can't accomplish that. When you become peaceful with yourself, you are much better equipped to handle life. You have also been coping with the cumulative stress of change, which is difficult; everyone resists. And you're learning to be self-reliant instead of turning to others."

I listened carefully and realized I wasn't quite there yet: obviously, it was taking me longer to adjust to single life.

Or was it just that it was an easy answer for me? Readily available, so I accepted his explanation? Learning to be alone was part of it, but not the whole of it. Another therapist explained later that the panic attacks were a delayed reaction to realizing just how dangerous the years with Cooper had been.

"Am I going to have to go back to the psych ward?" My voice shook.

"It might help to be admitted for a short time."

"I feel panicky but don't want to go back. Do you believe that I can make it on my own?"

"I have no doubt you'll get through this. I'm going to write you a prescription for Prozac to treat your depression. It can take up to six weeks before you feel results."

"Will that interfere with Xanax?"

"They can be taken simultaneously. You're going through a very difficult period. As time passes, you'll have only an occasional need for Xanax."

As we drove home, my thoughts turned to my stay at Richard Young Hospital when I was in my late twenties.

I was confused and had no direction. I was dissatisfied in my marriage and felt guilty because Boots was a good man. Everyone who knew him loved and respected him. I would get the blame if our marriage failed. Unresolved childhood and adolescent issues had contributed to my anguish. I had missed crucial stages of development throughout my teens and hadn't established an identity nor independence.

Seven years after my marriage to Boots, I finally went through a separation from my mother, finding fault with her and questioning our relationship. She interfered and disapproved of so many of the choices I made. I started seeing a psychiatrist, Dr. St. John.

After a few months of counseling, I broke down during a session in his office. "I feel like I'm losing my mind. I need to get away and figure out what's wrong with me."

The doctor looked surprised. "Don't be so hard on yourself; look how far you've come since we started."

"No, I can't do this," I sobbed.

He arranged for my admittance. I don't know if Boots understood, but as always, he was very supportive and drove me to Richard Young. He kissed me and asked, "Do you have everything you need?"

I nodded. "Tell the kids I love them."

As frightening as it was to check myself into Ward 7, I had to figure out why I was so anxious and depressed.

I was not on the same floor with the extreme cases. The doors were not locked; I could have checked out at any time. But I had issues to tackle, and these issues are painful for me to bring up. I had buried them for years which wasn't helping me.

Ben and I met when I was in high school and started dating after I graduated. He was smart, very masculine, and tall with broad shoulders; we were so attracted to one another. He asked my father for my hand in marriage, and I felt he was the one. I loved Ben as much as any nineteen-year-old can be in love. His family didn't meet Mom's standards; they ran a small Mom and Pop grocery store on the wrong side of town. She felt her daughter could do oh so much better. I can't remember the details, but Ben backed away and was extremely hurt and angry at me. They say, "The best revenge is a massive success." Well, Ben showed my mom: he became a successful doctor.

So, I settled for Boots and ended up in a loveless marriage. When I had my first child, I was discouraged that she turned out to be a carbon copy of my flawed self. The poor child was very lovable, though.

Within a couple of short years, my sister Carol announced her marriage to a man that Mother disapproved of. Mom turned the entire family against her, thinking that Carol would choose us over Paul. That didn't happen, and we lost her. All this caused much stress compounded with anxiety. It was like being pulled in ten different directions. I felt my only option was to check myself in.

I was shown to a small sterile room – no window, two beds, and a plain white dresser. I made friends easily. The staff was nice, comforting, and patient. With daily therapy, both one-on-

one and group, I made some headway and finally began the long overdue separation from my mother, which normally takes place during the teen years. Although still struggling, I told Dr. St. John that I wanted to go home two weeks after my admittance.

As Boots went to get the car, a nurse waited with me. I confided, "I'm ashamed that I was a patient here. What will my friends say?"

"No one knows what the future holds," she replied. "Your friends could be patients here someday. It can happen to anyone, and that includes me."

The fear that I might need to return to Ward 7 has haunted me during stressful times. As always, I had unconditional love from Diane and unwavering loyalty from Rachel. I increased my exercise regime and began walking three miles a day. The anxiety attacks continued.

At a morning Toastmasters meeting I worked myself into a state: sweating, pounding heart – *I* had to leave. Therefore, the member I rode with also had to gather her things, say her goodbyes, and see to my unexplainable fears.

One afternoon Diane stopped by to do my hair. While the curling iron was warming up, I said, "I think I need to sell this house. There are too many memories. It's too big, and I'm afraid at night."

As my twenty-four-year-old daughter worked her magic on my hair, she also worked on my psyche. "It's not the house, Mom. It's you. You're rid of Cooper, and now you're letting Aunt Sybil back in. Don't replay critical tapes."

Diane was right. Aunt Sybil had been a shadow at my back for far too long.

What I didn't address with either psychiatrist or anyone, was an issue that had evolved in my teens: panic attacks. I was too embarrassed to talk about it. The thought of not being in control scared me. I never feared the loss of my eyesight like I feared these attacks. I didn't understand them. There were times I could get on a plane or walk into a crowded room without a hitch. Other times it was hellish. I reduced the anxiety by sitting near a door, in the back of an airplane, or the back row at the crowded Synagogue.

I believe the panic attacks were a result of the cruel and patronizing remarks aimed at me in my childhood, and my parents never defended me. That is also when I learned I had to be flawless to fit in and to be loved. I thought I had worked through the anxiety during my years with Cooper, but I did border on the edge of hysteria. It just manifested differently. During an attack when he would disappear into the trees or drop me at my house, my way of coping was to call friends or clean in a frenzy. It wasn't safe for him to see the other side of me.

Since those years, for the most part, I have learned to enjoy my life. I keep busy working, exercising, and reading, don't dwell on the negative, and trust in myself a lot more. I pray. A lifetime of verbal and emotional abuse can't be erased overnight, if at all. On the other hand, my past has made me a stronger and more resilient person.

Thirty-four

My best friend, Rachel and I sat at a well-lit table at Gorat's treating ourselves to filets that melted in our mouths. I was happy to have some one-on-one time with her. She has a wide circle of friends, and at first, I was unsure if there would be room for me. But we always found time for one another.

"Thanks for eating here," I said, savoring a piece of garlic toast.

"It's one of my favorites, but if I want to keep the bills paid, McDonald's is our once-a-month splurge." She put a dollop of sour cream on her baked potato.

"How is everything going?" I asked.

"Pretty well, except that I'm sick of Frank. He pays minimum child support and bitches every time he writes a check. He still has delusions of non-responsibility; just like when we were together. That's not even the half of it. I sold him the house on Cane Street on condition that he take care of the legal paperwork. Since Mr. Stud was sleeping with a county judge and a paralegal, he said, 'It's as good as done.'"

I looked up, "He didn't follow through?"

"Are you kidding? His shenanigans are giving me an ulcer."

"You rarely hear of an amicable divorce," I said.

The waitress topped our coffee and left the check.

"How about you? Any Mr. Micklin's on the horizon?"

I laughed aloud. "No! I have shelves full of books and Niki curled up beside me."

Rachel stared me down. "Come on. No prospects?"

"If fate sent an intelligent, interesting, independent, financially secure man as they say in the personals, I would consider him."

"Have you thought about the Internet?" Rachel asked as we crossed the parking lot.

"No. I don't want to end up with another Cooper."

She ducked into the car and opened my door, pulled the compact from her purse, and repaired her lipstick. "Are you going to your high school reunion?"

"I haven't seen my classmates in years. We'll have nothing in common." I could see it now, Ruth Ann on one side of me raving about the new shed she and her husband built in their back yard, and Lee on my other side revealing the unpleasant details of a recent visit to the vet with their precious dog, Buddy, after he swallowed a Lego.

"There might be an old flame looking for a hot date," Rachel urged.

"There are no old high school flames." Weary of discussing my social life, I said, "I'll think about it." Did I want to bother with the reunion? Who would take me? Who would see that I arrived home safely?

I called Annette, chair of the planning committee, to let her know I would not be going. She urged me to attend, mentioning there would be a few single men present. One of them was Howie Kahn, who was divorced and had retained his physique and had a full head of salt-and-pepper hair: a bonus in the group of balding, portly men. We had a good laugh about that, and I decided it might be fun to reminisce about boy/girl stairs and Peony Park dances, and see how well – or not – everyone had aged; who had hair. I arranged transportation with Diane and mailed my reservation on Monday.

The evening of the reunion, I dolled up in an Anne Klein, white silk blouse, black satin skirt, and black and white striped heels. Diane swept my hair back in a more youthful style, securing the sides with pearl embellished combs. I wore my new shell shaped black onyx ring which symbolized my freedom from Cooper. Borsheim's had exchanged it for my wedding band. No more nostalgia for me.

Our class celebrated the reunion in a spacious banquet room at the Hilton Hotel. Annette knew I didn't want to be lost in the center of the room, floundering in the dim lighting trying to find a chair to plop into or a wall to guide me and took me under her wing. Our table included her husband and three other couples. Making sense of the sea of faces greeting me took total concentration, "I remember you, Dick – English – Miss Turpin's class; yanking my hair and getting *me* into trouble."

After dinner, Annette spotted Howie Kahn standing alone, leaning against the wall, sipping a drink, and scanning the crowd. She urged me to say hello. I mustered up the courage and slowly crossed the room. Although Howie and I barely knew each other in high school, we managed to strike up a conversation. He offered to buy me a drink. On the way to the bar, we passed Lisa Metz's table. She invited us to sit down and said, "Renee, you're the best-looking woman in our class."

"Thank you," I blushed. The irony of Lisa's comment took me back to eighth grade.

I was fourteen, attending a Beth El Synagogue Youth Group dance. Lisa, the "it" girl of the class, popular with both boys and girls, twirled around the floor in a pink taffeta dress. All the boys were in love with her. She was vibrantly pretty, naturally blonde, smart, and just as sweet as she was beautiful.

I was a wallflower showing no inclination to blossom. At the end of the evening, I cried to my mother. "It's not fair. All the boys want to dance with Lisa. I want to be her."

Mom comforted, "You're a late bloomer; your time will come. They will tire of the girls they're dancing with now and welcome a fresh face."

Mom was right. When I was seventeen, the boys began to notice me.

During high school, we had a Jewish sorority made up of some arrogant participants. The members were jealous of Lisa's beauty, personality, and popularity and blackballed her. They had no empathy for the emotional toll it took on her. Their cruelty made a lifelong impression on me.

After the reunion, Howie Kahn and I dated occasionally. One evening we were indulging in dessert at a coffee shop. He appeared uncomfortable as he stared out the window at the empty parking lot while inhaling apple pie ala mode. Why won't he look at me, I wondered. Am I wearing too much rouge? Is my mascara smeared?

"A penny for your thoughts," I said.

"Well…" Howie hesitated, choosing his words carefully. "My daughter asked if we were still an item."

"And?"

"My favorite sport is biking. I want someone to ride with me. You can't see well enough."

Howie's dumping me; make him say the words. "What do you mean?"

Still refusing eye contact, he leaned over his dessert to take a bite. Ice cream dropped in his lap. He whined a curse and dipped his napkin in his water glass to clean the spot, leaving a wet spot on his crotch. "I can't date you anymore."

Suddenly I had 20/20 vision and saw Howie for who he was. Why not just admit that he didn't want to see me? Blaming it on my eyesight was a cop-out. My resilience surprised me. His words stung but didn't injure. I no longer needed every man to be attracted to me. At least he'd repaired my backyard gates.

Even though I'd shrugged off dating to Rachel, men were still on my mind.

I was at the Rumor Mill for my Saturday beauty treatment. As the stylist walked me to the dryer, I waved at my former P.I., Starr Allen. She was spraying a customer's hair. I held my breath as I walked through the fog. From under the dryer, I watched a parade of pompous, stuck-up women chasing the flawless image.

Starr, with Wal-Mart glasses on the tip of her nose, flipped my dryer hood and shouted over the noise, "Renee, are you dating anyone?"

Several dryer helmets rose above ear level. My face turned red.

"Not now," implying that my dance card was ordinarily full.

Turning to acknowledge someone, she cackled at an aside. Facing me again, she yelled in my ear, "You've got to meet this marvelous man, Ron Steindorf. Isn't that Jewish?"

Without waiting for my response, she enthused, "He's divorced. His ex-wife has custody of their child. How that happened, I'll never know. Stop at my station when you're finished."

Sporting my new do, I made it to her chair without tripping over anyone's pumps, and Starr jotted down a phone number.

I hurried home to dial "Mr. Wonderful." The recommendation of a P.I. should be trustworthy.

"Ron?" I said brightly, enthusiastically.

"Yes." He answered just as animatedly.

"Starr Allen gave me your number."

"Starr and I have been friends for a long time," he said. "Did you meet her at work?"

Nice voice. "You might say that. I was divorced several years ago. We met then."

"I'm a casualty also. I have an eight-year-old son I don't get to see much."

"That's tough."

"I want to meet you," he said. "How's tomorrow?" We set the time for 2:00 p.m.

He must have found my voice appealing. What should I wear?

There was no way to anticipate the man standing at my door. It was a far cry from what I had imagined from his terrific voice. I later learned that he had been good looking until a botched facelift disfigured him. With high arching eyebrows, he had a permanent look of surprise on his face, like a clown. He appeared to be experiencing an identity crisis. Like Sonny Crockett in Miami Vice, Ron wore a white V-neck T-shirt – chest hair sprouting out of the top – a black sports jacket, jeans, and a thick gold chain. His thinning red hair with gray roots was pulled back in a Steven Segal ponytail. *I'm going to kill Starr.* As we drank coffee, he shared his career bio, checking them off with his long thin fingers, "I'm a licensed counselor, cosmetologist, realtor, and ordained priest of the Greek Orthodox Ukrainian Church. I once owned several beauty shops."

"Is that how you and Starr met?"

"Yes, I hired her straight out of beauty school."

Birds of a feather, I thought. Starr and Ron had a laundry list of jobs on their résumé.

Looking over the rim of his coffee cup, Ron said, "You're pretty and smart. I'm going to marry you."

Red flag! Cooper's words to me on our first date.

I laughed, "You don't even know me." He was coming on like a freight train. I found him unappealing and the swiftness of his proposal preposterous, but attention was attention.

"You forget I'm a licensed therapist. I received my Ph.D. from the University of Minnesota. Reading people is my job."

Ron didn't sweep me off my feet.

He prided himself on writer's wit and blandished me with poetry. The pages went straight to the trash can. He phoned daily. Our only commonality was a passion for politics. At opposites sides, debating the issues on the phone was a welcome respite from my daily humdrum. At times, we butted heads. Plus, I didn't have to look at him.

Then two incidents occurred that peeled away Ron's façade. One afternoon he phoned after returning from his telemarketing job. I was in the middle of Chapter seven of a good book and asked if I could call him back. Later his answering machine repeatedly picked up. As the afternoon stumbled along, I knew that Ron was sulking because I didn't drop everything to talk. The psychologist was playing mind games. Old ploy, new player.

He wanted a costly Harley Davidson – not used, brand new. Another man who wanted a bike. I had mentioned how much I enjoyed riding with Cooper. Ron had no money. He hinted that I should buy him his fantasy ride. He could dream as much as he wanted; I would never again purchase a bike for anyone. I had no intention of getting serious but was willing to continue seeing him, rather than spend my nights alone.

One evening he took me to a Mexican restaurant and asked if I'd thought about buying the motorcycle that would put us on the road to freedom. I asked him what a legally blind woman was going to do with a bike. I expected his next request to be a sawed-off shotgun and an acreage!

His following question surprised me. "What are your dreams for the future?"

"My dreams? I'd like to publish a book."

Ron finished his burrito which looked like a loaf of bread smothered in hot sauce. He guzzled his margarita and waved to the waitress for another.

I pushed the cold rice and beans around on my plate and took a sip of water. I hadn't intended to elaborate, but I heard myself say, "I wrote a book on widowhood. The first draft, anyway, but so much was going on in my life at the time, I set it aside."

"Are you going to finish it now?" Ron asked, squeezing the lime in his fresh drink.

"No, there are other topics that I'm considering."

When I walked into the house, both phones were ringing – Rachel was on one line, Crystal on the other. Uneasy about this mystery man, Rachel said, "If you're going to date him, hire a private investigator to do a background check." Crystal was also worried that I knew very little about Ron.

Their doubts, added to my experience with Cooper, compelled me to take a closer look.

I employed a detective. Not Starr. I met with him at my home and shared my limited information. Three days later he returned with a thick notebook. Ron Steindorf, a.k.a. John Steiner, a.k.a. Ron Stein, a.k.a. John Dorfman had a thirty-year criminal history. He lied about the University of Minnesota. He had no Ph.D., nor was he a priest. He had never owned any beauty shops. The only thing he had ever possessed was a used car. Ron was a low-grade hustler. The investigation revealed that he had swindled two widows. They agreed to talk to me if I kept their information confidential and guaranteed their anonymity. One disclosed that she had given him six thousand dollars, and the other three thousand. Then he disappeared. Hiring the detective was the smartest money I'd ever spent. I called Ron to say that I couldn't continue to see him. He didn't give up easily. His trite poems arrived daily for six weeks. I never responded.

I don't believe Starr knew he was a criminal. She takes people at face value. She thought of me as lonely and unable to get out and meet men. Ron was a good friend of hers and down on his luck.

Kim, an acquaintance, put on her matchmaker's hat. She knew a divorced man who had emigrated from Israel. Perhaps it would be different with Ira. He was handsome: silver hair, dark eyes, personable, and spoke with an appealing foreign accent. Very sexy. He invited me to visit him for the holidays at his apartment in California. Kim encouraged me to go. She thought it would be a positive distraction after the Ron debacle.

It sounded tempting, but I finally listened to my inner voice, which warned, 'Wait. Get to know this guy first.' The desire for romance hadn't faded, but caution was my new companion. Ira called in January, ardent to begin our love story. But first, would I "lend" him $7,500 to pay off his debts? Then he would move to Omaha and live with me.

Wow, lucky me! This time NO came without hesitation from that place where self-respect and hope coexist with wisdom from healed wounds. It was a liberating turning point.

I was beginning to make discoveries about myself. The more time I spent alone, the more I realized that I didn't need or want a man to fill the void.

Thirty-five

My friend, Monte, invited me to a wedding in which he would be best man. Playing cupid in a tuxedo, he had this wild idea to set up the groom's soon-to-be-divorced father with a new romantic interest. Carl was the father. I was the romantic interest.

He was stumbling through a rocky divorce, a process in which both parties have someone to blame at every stage of contention. I wasn't keen on hearing separation horror stories since I was sure I could match every skirmish or provide even bloodier anecdotes of my own. Monte prevailed, saying that Carl was a cool guy, and easy on the nerves.

This odd couple, me the book nerd, and Carl, the wanna be wood carver, sat next to one another during the reception. He was average height, paunchy, and bald and had a round Charlie Brown head. His glasses were too big for his face, with thick lenses that magnified his pale blue eyes and constantly slid down his nose. His first question was, "Do you like to camp?"

"No," I chuckled, picturing myself pitching a four-person tent inside-out.

An awkward moment passed. Carl smiled, "Do you like to fish?"

"No," I said, imagining trying to poke a squirming, slimy worm with a barbed fish hook.

I said, "Do you like to read?"

"If they're the movie version," Carl said.

I rolled my eyes, thinking, "I hope not westerns." It turns out Carl's favorites were Steven Segal action films. I wasn't trying to impress him and didn't care that we were like night and day. If he didn't like me, he didn't have to see me.

We ate, had cake, and toasted the bride and groom. From our table, we watched couples sway and shuffle and kids hokey-pokey on the dance floor. Carl introduced me to many of his family members who stopped by our table. He loved to tell stories; they were genuine life stories. Monte checked in on me from time to time.

On the drive home, he asked, "So … what do you think?"

I didn't tell him what I actually thought, which was a *nebbish*, or dull. A simple man. A man with more intelligence and masculinity was what would gain points with me. Instead, I shrugged and gave the diplomatic answer, "He was nice, but I don't picture us on a gondola in Venice accompanied by a violinist."

"Monte said, 'He thought you were a sweetheart.'"

The young matchmaker had our best interests at heart. If Carl called, and I believed he would, we would see where it went. If it didn't catch fire, I figured life was too short to try harder.

A week later, Carl and I went to dinner. Candle lit tables and interesting conversations goes a long way toward establishing a romantic relationship. We didn't have that, so romance didn't take. More important to us, platonic love built a firm foundation of friendship.

I enjoyed Carl; his down to earth good sense. He was completely at ease with his unschooled self in all kinds of mixed company. Status didn't impress him. It didn't matter if you were Warren Buffet or a transient on the street.

No matter how many times or what hour of the day I called, he always listened with patience and understanding. We were comfortable in our silences. We learned to move around each other easily and talk openly about our children's quandaries or not talk. He validated me when he thought I was right and always told me if he believed I was on the wrong track. Like the time I read him a scene in my memoir, and he quietly commented, "I don't feel like I'm in that room."

Carl existed in his own world – my garage, where he had a straight, narrow, dusty path through an accumulation of his clutter: woodworking tools, scrap wood, car parts, and half the broken furnishings became his as part of his divorce decree. On built-in shelves, you might find safety glasses, an open bag of charcoal briquettes, paint stripper next to a bottle of transmission fluid, and jumper cables hanging from a hook. His happy preoccupation with a new homemade project that he put a lot of love and planning into, often went unfinished. When he came through the garage door after hours of tinkering, his hands grimy, dirt under his fingernails, glasses coated with sawdust, he never failed to ask, "How are you today?" with warmth and sincerity. He cared deeply.

Several years into our friendship, Omaha had an ice storm. There were warnings on TV, but the frigid blast was more than anyone anticipated, rendering the roads unfit to travel and recommending people stay put. The autumn morning began with a steady rain that continued all day. By evening, a polar air mass moved through, turning the precipitation to a heavy wet snow. The wind increased, and the temperature dropped, freezing everything that was already soaked through. Ice-coated branches sagged and broke from their trunks falling over power lines, sending them sparking to the ground. The worst of the storm was the electricity going out city-wide, leaving an enormous number of households in the dark. That included my home, deactivating my security system and sending me into a panic. Because of my past with Cooper, having no alarm system terrified me. My unselfish friend, Carl, left his home where he had heat and lights and maneuvered the streets to stay with me. For eight frigid days, we huddled near the fireplace in my den, living by candlelight, lanterns, and take-out meals. Indoor camping. He arranged with his employer to go to work after sunrise, so I would not have to be alone in the dark. After the power came on again, he and his dog, Dempsey, returned to his home. If that's not friendship, what is?

We had nothing in common. I have an avid interest in politics; Carl didn't have a clue who was in office; didn't care. "Bunch of hustlers," he said. I love reading; he'd rather pick up a nine-pound hammer than a two-hundred-page book. He enjoyed parties and barbecues – Husker games with friends and relatives; I'm a homebody. None of that mattered. There was no more loyal friend than Carl.

I learned from him that there are people who aren't going to yell, judge, criticize me or put me down, just because I do things or think a little differently. That, despite my upbringing and my repeated victimization by Cooper, I am an acceptable person, no matter my choices and the outcome. I needed someone to know me. *The real me*. And not leave. That was the true gift Carl gave me.

Thirty-six

I stepped to the podium and looked at the blur of faces in the crowd, wishing I could make out features. All I could see were impressionistic representations like a painting in a museum. I was among a group of five that were asked to speak on behalf of the 40 million Americans who suffer with disabilities and were willing and able to be employed. On this day, our audience was a large group of executives from Mutual of Omaha Insurance Company. Loud chatter filled the auditorium as everyone entered and found friends and colleagues to join. Our objective was to champion the *abilities* of the physically disabled. I didn't need notes; I lived this life every day.

"Good Morning. My name is Renee Micklin. I'd like to start by thanking management for inviting me here.

"I was born with Retinitis Pigmentosa – a progressive eye disease. Today I'm legally blind.

"When I was little, I had night blindness, then my peripheral vision diminished; finally, depth perception failed me. Now, I can read only with the aid of very high-powered magnifiers.

"Years ago, I began a career as a speaker. My vision impairment often presents difficult

challenges in the business. One of my first engagements was at a bank in Lincoln. My new driver and I got lost and were late. As we searched for the woman who had hired me, I failed to notice an open flight of six steps and tumbled to the bottom. People rushed to help. Mortified, and trying to suppress tears and embarrassment, I declined their kindness. Both my pride and my body were bruised, and I needed to get up on my own.

"Cheryl and I went to the restroom, and she helped me wash the blood off my arm and repair my makeup. I was shaky and sore but was determined to speak at the scheduled times in the morning and afternoon.

"The pain in my right arm worsened as the day progressed. I could barely lift it to the podium and forget about carrying my briefcase. It's a good thing Cheryl was with me.

"Returning to Omaha, we stopped at the doctor's office. X-rays showed I had a badly torn ligament in my forearm. It took months to heal. I wanted to quit. It was my fourth fall that year. Instead of pride in my accomplishment, I berated myself for my handicap, which was totally beyond my control.

"Misconceptions about the visually impaired anger me. It is infuriating to be labeled mentally challenged.

Typically, when one sense is compromised the others get magnified. My daughter says I have the memory of an elephant and the nose of a bloodhound. Since I don't have the luxury of looking up phone numbers and addresses, I store a lot of information in my head. I rely on my memory to get through each day.

"With the loss of my vision, I not only lost one of my senses, but I also had to change the way I lived. Which proved to be very challenging. But I refuse to let blindness define me. The reality is, I have had to relearn everything, like using the remote or dialing a telephone. It might slow me down, but it doesn't stop me.

"Disabilities and prejudice tend to go hand in hand. In some instances, I've encountered people who didn't think I was qualified, simply because of my vision impairment. Of course, there are limits – I wouldn't make a good brain surgeon. I wouldn't even try. But I wish I had studied to be a linguist. I love languages.

"Those of us who live with a handicap don't want pity. We want respect and an equal opportunity to be a contributing member of society. Historically, the public has tended to isolate and segregate individuals with disabilities. If we have the skills for the job, we shouldn't be passed over. Put us to work. Help us prove our worth. I believe many doors will open for the disabled. Thank you."

Afterthought

At a time when I thought I had it all figured out, Diane changed everything saying, "All these years you've blamed Aunt Sybil for your damaged self-worth. But, it was your Mom. You're going to have to go there and admit the truth and quit worrying about being the bad daughter."

Her memories are limited: Doublemint gum, red nail polish, and Nanna teaching her and Abby to knit. No hugs or kisses. Then, when I'd talk about my hateful encounters with Aunt Sybil, Diane's thought was, "Where was your Mom?"

She was there.

Growing up, it seemed only natural to me that a mother and daughter have a bond and connection. So, my first reaction to Diane's words was shock. Then the realization came in slow motion like I was under water. I resisted her words and couldn't believe that something was wrong in my relationship with Mom. However, all my life I felt that I had rarely pleased her and that she found fault with me. With the shock, fragments of memory came to me accompanied by confusion.

I'll admit, the memories I have are almost like being an only child. I hardly ever played with my sisters. Still, that didn't seem unusual to me, as I was four years older than Joany and six years older than Carol. Our interests and friends were different.

Then came denial, and I tried to unearth evidence to support my disbelief. To protect the meaningful memories that I had, I reasoned, "*But there was the good Mom. She baked me a chocolate cake for an after school treat and stayed with the kids while I vacationed with Donald and was financially generous.*" I clung to those rosy images for my emotional well-being. It came with a cost, though: as good as the cake was, it did not erase the harsh words that I often heard, "*You are lazy and selfish. You think of no one but yourself.*"

I've learned that many of us unwittingly choose a partner with personality traits that are similar to our mother or father. Cooper possessed the same narcissistic characteristics as the women in my mother's family. At the time I married him, I had not worked through the abuse I'd suffered at the hands of the people who were supposed to love me the most; it wasn't surprising that I was attracted to someone with familiar qualities. As Sigmund Freud said, "What we don't resolve, we often repeat."

Living in an addictive love relationship was the result of being brought up in a household that lacked nurturing, empathy, and affection. I thought I was loved, but now I see it was conditional. I accepted that as normal, which followed me into my marriages. I thought that if I dressed right, looked nice, said the right thing, the love flowed.

I'm a work in progress to reprogram and un-do the damage done throughout my childhood and into adulthood. For years, I have fought to unravel my internal chaos. The truth is, I had carried a distorted self-image long before I met Cooper. The blueprint that I grew up with was that emotional abuse was equivalent to love.

As a graduate of the black and blue club, I will always carry scars. Not so long ago I'd second-guess a comment I'd made and worry that I had done or said something stupid and lost a friend or loved one. Making decisions or a having a confrontation may trigger self-doubt and I regress to the timid girl in Aunt Sybil's kitchen or the intimidated woman at Cooper's farmhouse; I might go back to being that ten-year-old sitting on the couch in the den, minding my own business, wondering if I was worthy of love when mom said, "You are lazy and selfish you think of no one but yourself."

My intention is not to dishonor my parents. I just had to travel down the long road to get to my healing place. And, I'm better off for having done so.

It's true I struggled for affirmation from my mother, but there was good in my life. The qualities I like most about myself I inherited from Dad: my love of reading, honesty, discipline in money matters, and not judging people by the size of their bank accounts.

I have finally begun my journey to trusting myself. My life is rich with promise and positive people. I don't know what tomorrow will bring, but I'm confident that I have the chutzpah to meet the challenge.

Made in the USA
Las Vegas, NV
30 June 2021